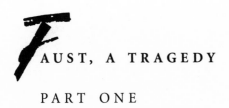# FAUST, A TRAGEDY

PART ONE

JOHANN WOLFGANG VON

Goethe

Faust

A TRAGEDY

PART ONE

A new translation by Martin Greenberg

Yale University Press New Haven and London

Jacket illustration: *Faust* by Emil Nolde, © Nolde-Stiftung Seebüll.

Designed by Nancy Ovedovitz and set in Minion type by DEKR Corporation. Printed in the United States of America by Vail-Ballou Press, Binghamton, New York.

Library of Congress Cataloging-in-Publication Data

Goethe, Johann Wolfgang von, 1749–1832.
    [Faust. 1. Theil. English]
    Faust, a tragedy. Part 1/Johann Wolfgang van Goethe ;
    a new translation by Martin Greenberg.
      p. cm.
    ISBN 0-300-05655-9 (cl.)
    ISBN 0-300-05656-7 (pbk.)
    I. Greenberg, Martin, 1918–   II. Title.
PT2026.F2G77 1992
832'.6—dc20   92-13753
                                                         CIP

10   9   8   7   6   5   4   3   2   1

For Paula, yet again

All of us live life, few have an idea about it.
—Goethe

CONTENTS

*T*RANSLATOR'S PREFACE

German nationalism, which ended its career of destruction by bringing about the destruction of Germany itself, also did its worst with the greatest work of Germany's greatest poet. As Nicholas Boyle writes,* it turned Faust, whose life from beginning to end is one shipwreck after another, into a hero

> who, driven by the tragic necessity of his "striving," "had to" shatter the limited, Catholic and therefore un-German world of Gretchen in order [in Part Two] to scale the heights of pagan classical culture, and to turn at last to useful work on behalf of the people ("Volk"). Although this regrettably involved murders, these were tragically, or historically, necessary and Faust had none the less, or therefore, deserved redemption. This grotesque travesty of Goethe's subtle poem was sanctified by the invention of the term "Faustian" (*das Faustische*) to describe modern humanity since the Renaissance, striving upward, especially in Germany, and through the toils of necessary guilt, towards some indeterminate collective goal, or possibly no goal at all. The nationalist interpretation of *Faust* culminated in Oswald Spengler's application of his name to a whole category of human history (*The Decline of the West*). By this course, alas, even *Faust* became a tributary to the ideology of National Socialism. However, Marxist interpretations, particularly those of Georg Lukács, use much the same conceptual apparatus and make much the same assumptions about the structure and intentions of the text.

* In his very superior commentary on *Faust: Part One* (Cambridge: Cambridge University Press, 1978), p. 129.

Goethe subtitled *Faust* a tragedy. In a work so profoundly unclassical, *anti*-classical, so varied in its matter, so large, so puzzling in its suggestions, this has little meaning. He might just as well have called it a comedy (though never a divine comedy). And indeed a few days before he died, in his last letter, he referred to *Faust* as "these very serious jokes." There is a tragedy in *Faust,* of course, in *Faust: Part One* that is; but its protagonist is Gretchen. Gretchen is tragic because, as she tells her lover in the last scene, she *must* die, it is the inescapable consequence of what she has done. She knows this in her simplicity as one who inhabits without question the old traditional moral-religious world. Anna Karenina later on, in the second half of the nineteenth century, is another such tragic protagonist. She, however, isn't simple but sophisticated; she knows she must die in spite of her sophistication, in spite of herself she still draws her vital breath from the old religious world.

For Faust, who has left that world behind, there are no inescapable consequences. He says so almost in his first words:

> I'm not bothered by a doubt or a scruple,
> I'm not afraid of Hell or the Devil.

But he has nothing with which to replace the old belief-world—

> Who'll teach me what to seek, what to shun?

—except experience and ever new experience, his striving and searching that always ends in shipwreck. A whole tribe follows after Faust in the novels of the nineteenth and twentieth centuries; I think of Julien Sorel in *The Red and the Black,* any number of Dostoyevsky's characters, K. in *The Castle.* Ortega y Gasset, in his essay on Goethe in *The Dehumanization of Art,* says with true profundity about a poet who has evoked so many hollow profundities, that "he is the man in whom for the first time there dawned the consciousness that human life is man's struggle with his intimate and individual destiny—that is, that human life is made up of the problem of itself, that its substance consists not in something that already is—like the substance of the Greek philosopher and, more subtly but in the last analysis equally, that of the modern idealist philosopher—but in something which has to make itself, which, therefore, is not a thing but an absolute and problematical task." And some pages later, turning the light of this observation on Goethe's literary works: "An enormous part of Goethe's work—his *Werther,* his *Faust,* his *Wilhelm Meister*—presents us with beings who go about the world searching for their inner destiny or . . . fleeing from it."

Faust, with his background in legend, his vaulting ambitions, his overweeningness, has the largeness of myth. He is one of the great figures of European literature. But as an Emily Dickinson poem declares,

> The abdication of belief
> Makes the behavior small.

And Faust's behavior at crucial junctures is small, indeed ignominious—Goethe never fails to view his protagonist critically, the chief agent of this criticism being Mephistopheles. (Goethe is in Faust, but how much of Goethe is in Mephistopheles!) How small Faust appears when he uses the bombast of sentimental love ("bosom," "soul") to ask Gretchen, coyly, to sleep with him and she answers him so straightforwardly. How small, how ignominious he appears beside Gretchen in the prison scene, she clothed in the tragic dignity of her self-judgment, he scurrying off with Mephisto.

Gretchen is one of the "little people" Mephisto promises Faust they are going to mix with first, when they fly off on his cloak into the world. Hers is the kind of "straitened life" his expansive spirit could hardly be expected to linger long in; before he meets her he has already rejected it as "not his sort of thing." Still, there is nothing straitened about her love for him; it is "eternal," to use the word he so desperately lays claim to to describe what he finds ultimately indescribable, his feeling for her. His desperation is genuine—the claim isn't only the self-deception Mephistopheles jeeringly calls it. But Faust is unable to sustain the claim. At the end, entering the prison in which she is awaiting execution, he exclaims how "all her crime was love, the brave, the illusory." Love for him is now illusory. The Voice from Above declaring Gretchen saved, not lost, isn't the

Lord's voice—the theology in *Faust* is one of Goethe's serious jokes. It is an absolute pronouncement by the poem itself which retorts upon Faust as well as Mephistopheles. At the end of *Faust: Part One* Faust hasn't lost his bet with Mephisto, he hasn't surrendered to "ease." Nevertheless, how very much a loser he is looking in his "Faustian" strivings.

Goethe called translators "busy go-betweens praising as adorable a beauty only glimpsed through veils; they provoke an irresistable desire in us for the original." However, his own *Faust*, in English, has not afforded the reader delectable glimpses. Though translated many times, it has been done into an unreal language of tortured rhymes and tortured syntax, the strangeness of the work made to seem insane by the grotesquerie of the English. Since the middle of the century there have been a few attempts at free-verse translations, which have the negative virtue of avoiding grotesqueries though not insipidities; they are lifeless and flat. Some recent verse translations have also wished to avoid unnatural language; the syntax is no longer tortured but broken-backed.

The verse in *Faust*, with its great variety of meter and rhyme, is remarkable for its variety of tone and style: dramatic, lyrical, reflective; farcical, ironical, pathetic; vernacular-simple and vernacular-coarse; colloquial and soaring. And though *Faust* sounds so many different notes, in an ultimate sense, as the work of one of the world's greatest, most inveterate lyrical poets, it is all lyrical, one great song. If a translation is to catch something of this and produce a poem in English (though not an English poem) that gives pleasure to the reader, it must be a translation into our English as it rings in life, our living American speech. That has been my aim. Aiming at that, I have used a free-ranging diction, meters looser, often, than those Goethe uses, and a much looser rhyming made up of half rhymes, assonance, and consonance; of course full rhymes, too, when they come naturally.

The fine Goethe scholar Barker Fairley says about *Faust* that "there is perhaps no other poem in modern literature of comparable length and complexity that stays so close to the vernacular."* Our English literature is classical down to its very foundations—using the word *classical* in its largest sense. Compare *Faust* with a great English romantic work, Wordsworth's *Prelude* for example, and see how orderly, elevated, harmonious—in a word, classical—*The Prelude* appears beside the Gothic plainnesses, irregularities, and homely detail, all the popular movement, to be found in *Faust*. Perhaps a translation of *Faust* can hope to succeed at last by drawing on the popular and colloquial resources which the American vernacular has in such abundance, as well as on the power of elevated expression of American English.

In making this translation I have gotten help wherever I could find it, from other translations, *Faust* commentaries, the *Faust* criticism. Barker Fairley's prose translation has been particularly helpful to me. As prose, it has a very limited aim; but the prose is Professor Fairley's, perspicuous, straightforward, easy.

I am most grateful to Professor Cyrus Hamlin of the Department of Comparative Literature of Yale University for his general critique of the manuscript, from which I profited greatly. A stay at the Rockefeller Foundation's Bellagio Study and Conference Center, with its ideal working conditions, made possible a big push forward in the work. I am glad to express my gratitude to the Foundation.

Last but hardly least, I wish to thank those who kept my spirits up with their encouragement. The history of failure with translations of *Faust* into English is daunting. Without the constant encouragement, reading and re-reading, and prompt, clear judgments of my wife, Paula Fox, I should have faltered. Ellen Graham of Yale University Press again provided the kind of editorial support I used to think one could expect from editors only in heaven. My thanks, too, to my friends Irving Howe and Gunther Stuhlmann, who read parts of the translation while it was in the making and cheered me on.

---

* *Goethe's Faust: Six Essays* (Oxford: Clarendon Press, 1953), p. 47.

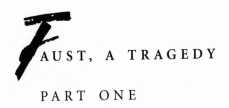

FAUST, A TRAGEDY

PART ONE

DEDICATION

Come back, have you, you figures shifting, spectral,
Whom I first dimly glimpsed in my young prime?
Try, shall I, this time, to hold on to you all?
Old ghosts, still able, are you, to exert your charm?
But how you crowd around me—I surrender!
And as you rise up out of mist and vapor,
The magic air that breathes around your shapes
Wakes old emotions from my youth, old hopes.

What scenes you bring back, days high-spirited and happy,
Dear shadows start up, living, from the dust,   10
First love, young friendships, like some ancient story
All but forgotten, revive for me, and griefs
Revive, and sighing I retrace life's labyrinthine,
Wandering course, naming the friends whom Fortune
Cheated of golden hours and hurried away
Into the darkness before me, out of the day.

They will not hear it, what's about to follow,
Those hearts who were the first to hear me sing,
All that brave company are scattered now,
Their loud vivas have long ceased echoing;   20
My song is poured out to the anonymous crowd,
Whose very praises fill me with misgiving.
Among those my verses once gave such delight,
If any live, they've long been lost to sight.

And a yearning, unfelt, unroused for so long,
For that somber spirit world, seizes me,
Like an Aeolian harp my renewed song
Trembles into sound uncertainly,
A shudder shakes my frame, my eyes brim over till
My too strict heart, relenting, is turned gentle;   30
All that's around me, mine, looks leagues away,
And what went glimmering is reality.

PRELUDE IN THE THEATER

Manager, Poet, Clown

MANAGER. You two who've always stood by me
When times were hard and the playhouse empty,
What do you think we can expect
From this tour of ours through German country?
I'd like so much to please the crowd,
For they're really so easy-going, so patient;
The posts are up, the floorboards laid,
And we've got to provide them some entertainment.   40
There they sit already, braced
For the wonders they are sure await them,
I know the way to tickle their taste
But I've never been in a fix like this one.
It's true what they're used to is pretty bad,
But Lord, what a terrible lot they've read.
So how surprise them with something lively and new,
A piece with some meaning that amuses them too?
I don't deny what pleases me most
Are droves of people descending on us,   50
Trying with all their might to squeeze
Through the strait gate to our Paradise,
When it's daylight still, not even four,
Using elbow and fist to get to the ticket seller
Like starving men rushing the baker's door—
For the sake of a seat prepared to commit murder.
Who works such a wonder on such a mixture
        of people? Why, the poet,
Him only. Fall to, then, dear colleague, and let's see you do it!
POET. Don't talk to me about that crowd of yours—
One look at them and my invention quite deserts me!   60
Oh shield me from those struggling, screaming hordes
Which swallow you up, against your will, completely!
No, lead me to some still, some dear retreat,

Only there is where a poet is happy,
There love and friendship, godlike, inspire and nurse
The precious gift that is the power of verse.
   Oh dear, what struggles up from deep inside us,
Syllables our lips shape slowly, haltingly
Into scenes effective or maybe ineffective,
Is drowned out in the present's hurlyburly;   70
Years must pass till, seen in time's perspective,
Its shape and soul shine forth as they are truly.
What's all flash and glitter lives a day,
The real thing's treasured by posterity.
CLOWN. Posterity! Oh that word—spare me it!
If all *I* ever thought of was the hereafter,
Who'd set the audience laughing in the present?
To be amused, that's their hearts' desire.
Having a clown on the stage who knows what his business is,
Is not to be sneezed at—it matters to know how to please.   80
When yours is the stuff to delight and enchant a whole
      theaterful,
You don't sourly mutter the public's a mob and it's fickle.
What you want's a full house, the sign out saying Standing
      Room Only,
For the bigger the house, the surer the response that you're
      after.
So be a good fellow and show us what drama should be,
Show us imagination, so various in her power,
And at her side show wisdom, good sense, feeling,
Show passion too—but mind you, show us some fooling!
MANAGER. But what's the first requirement? Plenty of action!
They're spectators, after all, they want to *see* something.   90
If you've got business going on every minute
That catches people's attention, that makes them all sit up,
Then you don't have to worry, they're yours, they're won
      over,
When the curtain comes down they'll shout "Author!
      Author!"

With the general public you've got to be general,
Something for everyone, that's how to please them all,
The last thing you want is to be classically economical!
In the theater today only scenes and set pieces do,
The way to succeed is to serve up a stew,
You can cook it up fast, dish it out easy too.   100
Now tell me, what good is your artistic unity—
The public will only make hash of it anyway.

POET.   But you don't understand—all that's just hackwork!
You don't stoop to such things if you're a true artist!
Those butchers you're fond of, those experts at patchwork,
Are your measure, I see, of what is a dramatist!

MANAGER.   Go ahead, scold me, I don't mind your censure,
To do a job right you use the tools that are called for.
Remember what hard wood you've got to split,
Consider the people for whom you write!   110
One's here because he's bored, another
Comes stuffed from eating a seven-course dinner,
But worst by far are the ones who come to us
Straight from reading the latest newspapers.
The crowd arrives here distracted, distrait,
Thinking of this and that, not of a play,
The reason they come is mere curiosity,
The ladies display their shoulders and finery,
Put on a great show without asking a salary.
Oh, the dreams poets dream in their ivory tower!   120
Flattered, are you, to see the house full?
Well, take a good look at our clientele,
The half vulgar and loud, half unmoved and sour;
One's mind's on his card game after the play,
Another's on tumbling a girl in the hay.
It's for people like that you fools torture the Muses?
Listen to me: You'll never go wrong
If you pile it on, pile it on, and still pile it on.
Bewilder, confound them with all your variety,
The public's the public, they're a hard lot to satisfy.   130

But goodness, you seem so worked up to me!
What's wrong? I can't tell if it's anguish or ecstasy.
POET. Go and find yourself some other lackey!
You expect the poet, do you, frivolously
To throw away, for your sweet sake alone,
His highest right from Nature as a man?
How does he teach humanity feeling?
Conquer the chaos of the elements?
I'll tell you, by the music pealing
Forth from his breast orphically,   140
Which then by reflux back on him returning
Reverberates as Nature's deep-voiced harmony.
When Nature winds life's endless strand
Indifferently on the bobbin, when
The hubbub of her countless creatures
Makes one continual buzz and hum,
Who melodizes her monotonous drone
And makes all move in living measures?
Who calls each mute particular
To sing its part in the general chorus,   150
In a glorious concord of myriad voices?
Who links our passions to wild tempests,
Our solemn moods to fading sunsets?
Scatters all the flowers of the springtime
To make a carpet for young love to walk on?
Twines green leaves, meaningless and ordinary,
Into a crown so greatness may be glorified?
Assures us of Olympus, unites in due order the gods?
That revelation of man's powers, the poet, does!
CLOWN. Then go on and use them, your marvelous powers!   160
Go at your business of making verses
The way you go at a love adventure:
A chance encounter, you're attracted, linger,
And little by little you find you're caught;
You're so happy, later you're not;
First you're enraptured, then it's pure misery,

And before you know it it's a whole history.
That's how to do it, write your love story that way!
Jump right into life's richness and riot,
All of us live life, few have an idea about it,   170
And my, how it interests wherever you scratch it!
Color, confusion, a wild hurlyburly,
With a glimmer of truth amid errors' obscurity,
And there you have it: exactly the right brew
To refresh everyone, make them think a bit too.
Then the best of our youth will flock here to listen,
Gripping their seats in anticipation;
The sensitive soul will find in your play
Food to feed his melancholy;
One thing touches one man, another another,   180
The end result is, all discover
What's in their hearts. The young are still ready
To laugh at a good thrust, let their tears flow in pity,
Warmly respond to high aspirations,
Cherishing still their bright dreams and illusions.
You'll never please people who find everything
Is an old story, nothing more's to be done;
But the youth, still growing, still developing,
How they will thank you, every one!

POET. Then give me back *my* youth again,   190
When all was growing, changing with me,
When song after song gushed from my lips
Like a fountain flowing uninterruptedly,
When a morning mist still veiled the world
And a bud was a promised miracle,
When I plucked the thousand flowers that filled
The vales with their rich spectacle.
The nothing I owned was more than enough,
I hungered for truth, rejoiced in illusion.
Oh days of anguished happiness,   200
Of unsubdued, of purest passion,
Of burning hatred and burning love—
Oh give me back my youth again!

CLOWN. Youth, my dear colleague, you need in the following
    cases:
  When the enemy's crowding you hard in the fight,
  When pretty girls in summer dresses
  Kiss and squeeze you with all their might,
  When running hard, you glimpse in the distance
  The wreath that rewards the fleetest foot,
  When after the madly whirling dances   210
  You wear the night out draining your cup.
  But to sweep the old familiar harp strings
  Boldly, yet with charm and grace,
  To make by pleasing indirections
  For the end your drama's set itself—
  That's a job for you old fellows
  And for it we respect you all.
  Age doesn't make us childish, God knows,
  Just finds us the same old children still.
MANAGER. All this talking's quite enough,   220
  Now do something to some purpose!
  You waste your time in compliments
  And quite forget your proper service.
  And please—don't tell me you're not in the right mood,
  It never arrives if you hesitate timidly.
  You claim you're a poet, you and the likes of you,
  Then come on, produce it, your great poetry.
  You know what's wanted: good strong stuff,
  So deliver the goods—stop fussing about it.
  What's put off today still tomorrow's put off: 230
  You mustn't, believe me, lose even a minute.
  Resolution's a spirit that bravely
  Seizes occasion by the short hairs,
  It won't let go but hangs on grimly;
  Once committed, it perseveres.

  You know how on our German stage
  We're free to try whatever we please,
  So don't imagine I want you to save

Me money on paint and properties.
Hang out heaven's big and little lamps,   240
Scatter stars over the canvas sky,
Let's have fire and flood and dizzying steeps,
All sorts of birds and beasts—do the thing liberally.
And thus on a narrow platform you're able
To go all the way round Creation's great circle
At a brisk enough pace, yet deliberately as well,
From Heaven, through this our world, down to Hell.

PROLOGUE IN HEAVEN

The Lord. The Heavenly Host. Then Mephistopheles. The three Archangels advance to front.

RAPHAEL. The sun blares out his age-old music
        In contest with each brother sphere,
        Marching around and around, with steps of thunder,   250
        His appointed circuit, year after year.
        To see him lends us angels strength,
        But what he *is*, oh who can say?
        The inconceivably great works are great
        As on the first creating day.
GABRIEL. And swift, past all conception swift,
        The jeweled globe spins on its axletree,
        Celestial brightness alternating
        With shuddering night's obscurity.
        Against earth's deep-based precipices   260
        The broad-running ocean tides are hurled,
        And rock and sea together hurtle
        With the eternally turning world.
MICHAEL. And hurricanes, contending, roar
        From sea to land, from land to sea,
        Linking in tremendous circuit
        A chain of blazing energy.

The lightning bolt makes ready for
The thunderclap a ruinous way—
Yet Lord, your servants reverence   270
The stiller motions of your day.

ALL THREE. From seeing this we draw our strength,
For what You *are*, oh who can say?
And all your great works are as great
As on the first creating day.

MEPHISTOPHELES. Lord, since you've stopped by here again,
    wanting to know
How all of us are doing, for which we're grateful,
And since you've never made me feel *de trop*,
Well, here I am too with your other people.
I hope you will excuse my lack of eloquence,   280
Though this whole host, I'm sure, will think me stupid;
Coming from me, high-sounding sentiments
Would only make you laugh—that is, provided
Laughing was a thing that you still did.
About suns and worlds I don't know beans, what I
Know is, how men and women find it hard to live.
Earth's little god's shaped out of the same old clay,
He's the same queer fish he was on the first day.
He'd be much better off, in my opinion, without
The bit of Heavenly Light you dealt him out.   290
He calls it Reason, and the use he puts it to?
To act more beastly than beasts ever do.
To me he seems, begging Your Worship's pardon,
Like a long-legged grasshopper all of whose leaping
Only lands him back in the grass again chirping
The tune he's always chirped. And if only he'd
Stay put in the grass! But no! It's an absolute need
With him to creep and crawl and strain and sweat
And stick his nose in every pile of dirt.

THE LORD. Is that all you have got to say to me?   300
Is that all you can do, accuse eternally?
Is nothing ever right for you down there, sir?

MEPHISTOPHELES. No, nothing, Lord—all's just as bad as ever.
　　I really pity humanity's myriad miseries,
　　I swear I hate tormenting the poor ninnies.
THE LORD. Do you know Faust?
MEPHISTOPHELES.　　　　　　The Doctor?
THE LORD.　　　　　　　　　　My good servant!
MEPHISTOPHELES. You don't say! Well, he serves you in a
　　　　funny way,
　　Finds meat and drink, the fool, in nothing earthly,
　　The ferment in him drives him on incessantly,
　　He himself is half aware he's crazy;　　　　　　　　　　310
　　From Heaven he must have the brightest stars,
　　From earth the most ecstatic raptures,
　　And all that's near at hand or far and wide
　　Leaves your good servant quite unsatisfied.
THE LORD. If today he's still confused, a soul astray,
　　My light shall lead him into the true way.
　　When the sapling greens, the gardener can feel certain
　　Flower and fruit will follow in due season.
MEPHISTOPHELES. Would you care to bet on that? You'll lose, I
　　　　tell you,
　　If you'll just give me leave to lead the fellow　　　　320
　　Gently down my broad, my primrose path.
THE LORD. As long as Faustus walks the earth
　　I won't, I promise, interfere.
　　As long as man strives, he is bound to err.
MEPHISTOPHELES. Well thanks, Lord, for it's not the dead
　　　　and gone
　　I like dealing with. What I prefer, oh much,
　　Are round and rosy cheeks. When corpses come
　　A-knocking, pardon me, I'm out to lunch;
　　My way of working's the cat's way with a mouse.
THE LORD. So it's agreed, you have my full consent.　　　330
　　Induce this soul to defect from its true source
　　And if you're able, lead him along, Hell bent
　　With you, upon the downward course—

Then blush for shame when you find you must admit:
Stumbling along as he must, through darkness and confusion,
(A good man still knows which road is the right one.)
MEPHISTOPHELES. Of course, of course! Yet I'll seduce him
          from it
Soon enough. I'm not afraid I'll lose my bet.
And after I have won it,
You won't, I trust, begrudge me   340
My whoops of triumph, shouts of victory.
Dust he'll eat
And find that he enjoys it, exactly like
That old aunt of mine, the famous snake.
THE LORD. There too you may feel free, you have carte blanche.
You know, I've never hated fellows like yourself.
I find, of all the spirits of negation,
You railers the least trying to my patience.
Man's very quick to slacken in his effort,
What he likes best is Sunday peace and quiet;   350
So I'm glad to give him a devil—for his own good,
To prod and poke and incite him as a devil should.
[*To the Angels*] But you who are God's true and faithful
          children—
Delight in the world's wealth of living beauty!
May that which moves all, ever changing, living,
Ring you around with smiling love, benignly,
And the fitfulness, the inconstancy, of appearance,
Seize it in thoughts that raise it into permanence.
[*The Heavens close, the Archangels withdraw.*]
MEPHISTOPHELES. I like to see the Old Man now and then,
And take good care I don't fall out with him.   360
How very decent of a Lord Celestial
To talk man to man with the Devil of all people.

NIGHT

In a narrow, high-vaulted Gothic room, Faust, seated restlessly in an armchair at his desk.

FAUST. I've studied, alas, philosophy,
Law and medicine, recto and verso,
And how I regret it, theology also,
Oh God, how hard I've slaved away,
With what result? Poor fool that I am,
I'm no whit wiser than when I began!
I've got a Master of Arts degree,
On top of that a Ph.D.,   370
For ten long years, around and about,
Upstairs, downstairs, in and out,
I've led my students by the nose
To what conclusion?—that nobody knows,
Or ever can know, the tiniest crumb!
(Which is why I feel completely undone.)
   Of course I'm cleverer than these stuffed shirts,
These Doctors, Masters, Jurists, Priests;
I'm not bothered by a doubt or a scruple,
I'm not afraid of Hell or the Devil—   380
But the consequence is, my mirth's all gone;
No longer can I fool myself
I am able to teach men
How to be better, love true worth;
I've got no money or property,
Worldly honors or celebrity;
A dog wouldn't put up with this life!
Which is why I've turned to magic,
Seeking to know, by ways occult,
From ghostly mouths, many a secret;   390
So I no longer need to sweat
Painfully explaining what
I don't know anything about;
So I may penetrate the power

That holds the universe together,
Behold the source whence all proceeds
(And deal no more in words, words, words.)

O full moon, melancholy-bright,
Friend I've watched for, many a night,
Till your quiet-shining face   400
Appeared above my high-piled desk—
If this were only the last time
You looked down on my pain!
If only I might stray at will
Beneath your light, high on the hill,
Haunt with spirits upland hollows,
Fade with you in dim-lit meadows,
And soul no longer gasping in
The stink of learning's midnight lamp,
Bathe in your dews till well again!   410

But oh, unhappy man that I am,
Isn't this your familiar prison?
Damned musty-smelling hole in the wall
Where even the golden light of Heaven
Must struggle hard to force its way through
The dim panes of the stained-glass window.
Yes, here you sit walled in by books
Stacked up to the shadowy vault,
Books worm-eaten, covered with dust,
With rolls of paper, all smoke-blackened,   420
Pushed and wedged and stuck between them,
With vessels, flasks, retorts, and beakers
Filling all the shelves and drawers,
And adding to the dense confusion
Your family's ancient furnishings.
Call this a world, this world you live in?

Can you still wonder why your heart
Should tighten in your breast so anxiously?

Why your every impulse is stopped short
By an inexplicable misery?   430
Instead of the living house of Nature
God created man to dwell in,
Dust, mold, they are what surround you,
Dogs' bones, a human skeleton.

Escape outdoors! Breathe the fresh air!
And this strange book of secret lore
By Nostradamus' own hand—
What better help to master the secrets
Of how the stars turn in their orbits,
From Nature learn to understand   440
The spirits' power to speak to spirits.
Sitting here and racking your brains
To puzzle out the sacred signs—
What a sterile, futile business!
Spirits, I feel your presence around me:
Announce yourselves if you hear me!

[*He opens the book and his eye encounters the sign of the Macrocosm.*]

The pure bliss flooding all my senses
Seeing this! Through every nerve and vein
I feel youth's fiery, fresh spirit race again.
Was it a god marked out these signs   450
By which my agitated bosom's stilled,
By which my bleak heart's filled with joy,
By whose mysterious agency
The powers of Nature all around me stand revealed?
Am *I* a god? All's bright as day!
By these pure brush strokes I can see,
At my soul's feet, great Nature unconcealed.
And the sage's words—I understand them, finally:
"The spirit world is not barred shut,
It's your own mind, your dead heart!   460

Stand up unappalled, my scholar,
And bathe your breast in the rose of Aurora!"

[*He contemplates the sign.*]

How all is woven one, uniting,
Each in the other living, working!
How Heavenly Powers rise, descend,
Passing gold vessels from hand to hand!
On wings that scatter sweet-smelling blessings,
Everywhere they post in earth
And make a universal harmony sound forth!
Oh, what a sight! But a sight, and no more!   470
How seize you and hold you, infinite Nature?
Find the life-giving fountains, your breasts, that sustain
Both the earth and the heavens, breasts at which my breast,
So dried up, a desert, is yearning to nurse—
You flow, *over*flow, yet I go on thirsting in vain.

[*Morosely, he turns the pages of the book and comes on the sign of the Spirit of Earth.*]

What a different effect this sign has on me!
You, Spirit of Earth, are closer to me,
Already fresh lifeblood pours through every vein,
Already I glow as if from new wine—
Now I have the courage to dare   480
To go out into the world and bear
The ill and well of life, to battle
Storms, and when the ship splits, not to tremble.

How the air grows thick overhead—
The moon's put out her light,
The lamp flame looks like dying.
Vapors eddy and drift—
Red flashes, leaping, dazzle—
Fear, shuddering down from the vault,
Seizes me by the throat!   490

Spirit I have invoked, hovering near:
Reveal yourself!
How all my senses fumble toward, founder in
Never-experienced feelings!
Spirit, I feel I am yours, body and breath!
Appear! Oh, you must! Though it costs me my life!

[*He seizes the book and pronounces the Spirit's mystic spell. A red flame flashes, in the midst of which the Spirit appears.*]

SPIRIT. Who's calling?
FAUST. (*Averting his face*) Overpowering! Dreadful!
SPIRIT. Potently you've drawn me here,
    A parched mouth sucking at my sphere.
    And now—?
FAUST.   Oh, you're unbearable!   500
SPIRIT. You're breathless from your implorations
    To see my face, to hear me speak,
    I've yielded to your supplications
    And here I am.—Well, in a funk
    I find the superman! I come at your bidding
    And you're struck dumb! Is this the mind
    That builds a whole interior world, doting
    On its own creation, puffed to find
    Itself quite on a par, the equal,
    Of us spirits? Wherever is that Faust   510
    Who urged himself just now with all
    His strength on me, made such a fuss?
    You're Faust? The one who at my breath's
    Least touch, shudders to his depths,
    A worm who wriggles away in terror?
FAUST. *I* shrink back from you, abject and fearful?
    Yes, I'm called so, called Faust—your equal!
SPIRIT. I surge up and down
    In the tides of being,
    Drive forward and back   520
    In the shocks of men's striving!

I am birth and the grave,
An eternal ocean,
A web changing momently,
A life burning hotly.
Thus seated at time's whirring loom
I weave the Godhead's living gown.

FAUST. We're equals, I know! I feel so close to you, near,
    You busy spirit ranging everywhere!

SPIRIT. It's your idea of me you're equal to,   530
    Not me! [*Vanishes.*]

FAUST. [*Deflated*] Not you?
    Then who?
    Me, made in God's own image,
    Not even equal to you?
    [*A knocking*]
    Death! My famulus—I know that knock.
    Finis my supremest moment—worse luck!
    That visions richer than I could have guessed
    Should be scattered by a shuffling Dryasdust!

[*Wagner in dressing gown and nightcap, carrying a lamp. Faust turns around impatiently.*]

WAGNER. Excuse me, sir, but wasn't that   540
    Your voice I heard declaiming? A Greek tragedy,
    I'm sure. Well, that's an art that comes in handy
    Nowadays. I'd love to master it.
    People say, how often I have heard it,
    Actors could really give lessons to the clergy.

FAUST. Yes, when clergymen go in for acting—
    Something I have seen in more than one case.

WAGNER. Oh dear, to be so shut up in one's study,
    Seeing the world only now and then, on holiday,
    And only from far off, as if through a spyglass—   550
    How can one ever teach it what's the right way?

FAUST. You can't—unless you speak with feeling's own
    True voice, unless your words are from

The soul and by their spontaneous power,
Seize with delight the soul of your hearer.
But no! Stick in your seats, you fellows!
Paste bits and pieces together, cook up
A beggar's stew from others' leftovers,
Over a flame you've sweated to coax up
From your own little heap of smoldering ashes,   560
Filling with wonder all the jackasses,
If that's the kind of stuff your taste favors—
But you'll never get heart to cleave to heart
Unless you speak from your own heart.

WAGNER. Still and all, a good delivery is what
Makes the orator. I'm far behind in that art.

FAUST. Advance yourself in an honest way.
Don't try to be a performing ape!
Good sense, good understanding, they
Are quite enough, they are their own art.   570
When you have something serious
To say, what need is there to hunt
Around for fancy words and phrases?
All those speeches polished up
With bits and pieces collected out
Of every tongue and race, are about
As bracing as the foggy autumnal breeze
Swaying the last leaves on the trees.

WAGNER. Dear God, but art is long
And our life—lots shorter.   580
Often in the middle of my labor
My confidence and courage falter.
How hard it is to master all the stuff
For dealing with each and every source.
And before you've traveled half the course,
Poor devil, you have gone and left this life.

FAUST. Parchment, tell me—that's the sacred fount
You drink out of, to slake your eternal thirst?
The only true refreshment that exists

You get from where? Yourself—where all things start.   590

WAGNER. But sir, it's such a pleasure, isn't it,

    To enter into another age's spirit,

    To see what thinkers long before us thought

    And measure how far since then we have got.

FAUST. As far as to the stars, no doubt!

    Your history, why, it's a joke;

    Bygone times are a seven-sealed book.

    The thing you call the spirit of the past,

    What is it? Nothing but your own poor spirit

    With the past reflected in it.   600

    And it's pathetic, what's to be seen in your mirror!

    One look and I have to beat a quick retreat—

    A trash can, strewn attic, junk-filled cellar,

    At best it is a blood-and-thunder thriller

    Improved with the most high-minded sentiments

    Exactly suited for mouthing by marionettes.

WAGNER. But the world we're in! The hearts and minds of men!

    Surely all of us want to know about them.

FAUST. Yes, know as the world knows knowing!

    Who wants to know the real truth, tell me?   610

    Those few with vision, feeling, understanding,

    Who failed to stand guard, most unwisely,

    Over their tongues, speaking their minds and hearts

    For the mob to hear—you know what's been their fate:

    They were crucified, burnt, torn to bits.

    But we must break off, friend, it's getting late.

WAGNER. I love serious conversation; to improve

    One's mind so, I'd stay up all night gladly.

    But it's Easter Sunday, sir, in the morning,

    And perhaps I may ask you a question or two then, if you're

        willing?   620

    I've studied hard, yes, studied diligently,

    I know a lot, but still, I aim at knowing everything. [*Exit.*]

FAUST. [*Alone*] How such fellows keep their hopes up is a

        wonder!

Their attention forever occupied with trivialities,
Digging greedily in the ground for treasure,
And when they've turned a worm up—what ecstacies!

That banal, commonplace human accents
Should fill air just now filled with spirits' voices!
Still, this one time you've earned my thanks,
You sorriest of human specimens.   630
You snatched me out of the grip of a dejection
So profound, I was nearly driven off
My head. So gigantic was the apparition,
It made me feel no bigger than a dwarf—

Me, the one made in the very image of God,
Fully persuaded the mirror of eternal truth
At last lay in his reach, already basking in
The heavenly light and glory, all earthliness cast off;
Me, higher placed than the cherubim, imagining
His own strength already poured freely,   640
Divinely creative, through Nature's great body! Well, now
I must pay for it: a thunderous word and I am laid low.

No, I can't claim we are equals, presumptuously!
Though I was strong enough to draw you down to me,
Holding on to you was another matter entirely.
In that exalted-humbling moment of pure delight
I felt myself at once both small and great.
And then you thrust me remorselessly back
Into uncertainty, which is all of humanity's fate.
Who'll teach me what to seek, what to shun?   650
Yield, should I, to that burning desire of mine?
Alas, what we do as much as what's done to us
Cramps and obstructs our entire life's progress.

The noblest thoughts our minds are able to entertain
Are undermined by a corrupting grossness;

When we've managed a bit of the good of this world for
    ourselves
Then the better's dismissed as a fairy tale or confidence game;
Those radiant sentiments which were once life itself to us
Grow pale and expire in the glare of the world's busyness.

There was a time when bold imagination   660
Pitched her flight as high as God's own station,
But now that everything I took such joy in
Has shipwrecked for me in time's maelstrom,
She's quite content to cower in a narrow space.
In our heart of hearts Care has her nesting place
And there she does her worst,
Dithering nervously, poisoning pleasure and peace,
Masking herself as genuine concern
For house and home, for wife and children,
In fear of fire and flood, violence and mayhem;   670
You shrink back in terror from imagined blows
And weep over losing what you never in fact lose.

Oh no, I'm no god, only too well do I know it!
A worm's what I am, wriggling through the dust
And finding his nourishment in it,
Whom the wayfarer treads underfoot.

These high walls with their shelves and niches—
Dust is what shrinks them to a stifling cell;
This moth-eaten world with its trash and its trinkets—
It is the reason I feel shut up in jail.   680
And here I'll discover the things I most lack?
Devour thousands of books so as to learn, shall I,
Mankind has always been stretched on the rack,
With now and then somebody, somewhere, who's happy?
   You, empty skull there, smirking so, I know why!
Your brain, once as whirling as mine is,
Seeking the bright day, longing for truth,

Blundered about, lost in onerous darkness, just as wretchedly.
And all that apparatus—how I feel you are mocking me,
With your wheels and cylinders, cams, and ratchets!   690
I stood at the door, certain you were the key;
But the key, though cut intricately, couldn't unlatch it.
Great Nature, so mysterious even in broad day,
Doesn't let you unveil her, plead how you may.
And if she won't allow you one glimpse of her mystery,
You'll never compel her with all your machinery.

Old instruments I've never touched,
You're here, and why?—because my father used you.
And you, old scrolls, have gathered soot
For as long as the lamp's smoked on this table.   700
Much better to have squandered the little I've got
Than find myself sweating under its weight.
It's from our fathers, what we inherit,
To make it ours truly, we've got to earn it.
What's never used weighs like lead;
What's useful responds to a living need.

But why do I find I must stare in that corner,
Is that bottle a magnet enchanting my sight?
Why is everything all at once lovely and luminous,
Like woods when the moon's up and floods them
        with light?   710

Vial, I salute you, O rare, O precious!
And reverently bring you down from the shelf,
Honoring in you man's cunning and craft.
Quintessence of easeful sleeping potions,
Pure distillation of subtle poisons,
Do your master the kindness that lies in your power!
One look at you and my agony lessens,
One touch and my feverish straining grows calmer
And my tight-stretched spirit bit by bit slackens.

The glassy waters glitter before me,   720
My way is clear—into Ocean's immensity,
A new day is dawning, a new shore beckons.

A fiery chariot, bird-winged, swoops down on me,
I am ready to follow new roads through the ether,
Aloft into new spheres of purest activity.
An existence so exalted, a rapture so godlike—
Does the worm of a minute ago deserve it?
No matter. Resolution! Turn your back bravely
On the sunlight, sweet sunlight, of our earth forever!
Fling wide open those dark gates, defiantly,   730
Which the whole world skulks past with averted heads!
The time has come to disprove by deeds,
Because the gods are great, man's a derision,
To cringe back no more from that black pit
Whose unspeakable tortures are your own invention,
To struggle toward that narrow gate
Around which all Hellfire's darkly flaming,
To take resolutely the last step,
Even at the risk of utter extinction.

And now let me take this long forgotten   740
Crystal wine cup down from its case.
Once it shone at our family feasts,
Making the solemn guests' faces brighten
When it went round with the lively toasts.
The figures artfully cut in the crystal,
Which it was the duty of all at the table,
In turn, to make up rhymes about,
Then drain the cup at a single draught—
How they recall many nights of my youth!
But now there's no passing you on to my neighbor   750
Or thinking up rhymes to parade my quick wit;
Here is a juice that is quick too—to intoxicate,
A brownish liquid, see, filling the beaker,

Chosen by me, by me mixed together,
My last drink! Which now I lift up in festive greeting
To the bright new day I can see dawning!

[*He raises the cup to his lips. Bells peal, a choir bursts into song.*]

CHORUS OF ANGELS.
    Christ is arisen!
    Joy to poor mortals
    By their own baleful,
    Inherited, subtle   760
    Failings imprisoned.
FAUST.   What deep-sounding peals, what caroling voices
    Arrest the glass before I can drink?
    Is that solemn ringing already proclaiming
    The glorious advent of Easter week?
    Already intoning, choirs, are you,
    What angels' lips sang, oh comforting chant,
    High above the sepulcher's darkness,
    Certain assurance of a new covenant?
CHORUS OF WOMEN.
    With sweet-smelling spices   770
    We laid out the man,
    We, his most faithful ones,
    Here at the tomb;
    In linen we wound him
    And bound up his hair—
    Oh, what do we find now?
    Christ is not here.
CHORUS OF ANGELS.
    Christ is arisen!
    Blest is the man of love,
    He who in triumph passed   780
    Earth's hard and bitter test,
    Bringing salvation.
FAUST.   But why do you seek me out in my dust,
    You music of Heaven, mild and magnificent?
    Ring out where men and women are simple,

I hear your message but can't believe it—
And where belief's lacking, no miracle's possible.
The spheres whence those glad tidings come
Are not for me to try and enter—
Yet all's familiar from when I was young   790
And back to life I feel myself summoned.
Years ago the Heavenly Love
Flew down to me in the Sabbath stillness
And caught me in His strong embrace;
Oh, with what meaning the deep bells sounded,
Praying to Jesus, oh what bliss!
A yearning so sweet it was not to be fathomed
Drove me out to the woods and the fields,
Inside my soul a new world opened
And my cheeks were streaming with scalding tears!   800
Your song gave the signal for the sports we rejoiced in
When the holiday springtime gladdened the world:
Innocent childhood's remembered feelings
Hold me back from the last step of all.
O sound away, sound away, sweet songs of Heaven!
Tears fill my eyes, earth claims me again!

CHORUS OF DISCIPLES.

> He who was buried
> Is already ascended,
> The one who on this earth
> Lived most sublimely, then   810
> Rose up in glory
> So he may take part in
> The bliss of creating.
> But here on the earth
> *We* huddle afflicted;
> He has left us, his children,
> Desponding, behind—Master,
> Must we bewail your good fortune?

CHORUS OF ANGELS.

> Christ is arisen
> From the womb of decay,   820

Strike off your fetters
And shout for joy!
Who praise him with works
Of loving-kindness
By feeding the hungry,
By preaching him east and west,
By promising blessedness—
You have the Master near,
You have him here, right here!

OUTSIDE THE CITY GATE

All sorts of people out walking.

SOME APPRENTICES. Where are you fellows off to?   830
OTHERS. To the hunters' lodge—over that way.
FIRST BUNCH. Well, we're on our way to the old mill.
ONE APPRENTICE. The river inn—that's what I say.
SECOND APPRENTICE. But the walk there's not much of a pleasure.
SECOND BUNCH. And what about you?
THIRD APPRENTICE.   I'll stick with the rest of us
          here.
FOURTH APPRENTICE. Let's go up to the village. There, I can
          promise you
     The best-looking girls, the best-tasting beer,
     And some very good roughhousing too.
FIFTH APPRENTICE. My, but aren't you greedy!
     You'd like your hide tanned still a third time?   840
     I'll never go there, it's too scary.
SERVANT GIRL. No, no, I'm turning back, now let me be.
ANOTHER. We're sure to find him at those poplar trees.
FIRST GIRL. Is that supposed to make me jump for joy?
     It's you he wants to walk with, wants to please,
     And you're the one he'll dance with. Fine
     For you. But what's it to me, your good time?

THE OTHER. He's not alone, I know, today. He said
    He'd bring his friend—you know, that curlyhead.
A STUDENT. Those fast-stepping girls there, look at the heft of
        them! 850
    Into action, old fellow, we're taking out after them.
    Beer with body, tobacco with a bite,
    And red-cheeked housemaids in their Sunday best
    Are just the things to make your Hermann happiest.
A BURGHER'S DAUGHTER. Oh look over there, such nice-looking
        boys!
    Really, I think they are so outrageous,
    They have their pick of the nicest girls
    And instead they run after overweight wenches.
SECOND STUDENT. [*To the first*] Hold up, go slow! I see two more,
    And the pair of them dressed so pretty, so proper. 860
    But I know that one! She lives next door,
    And she, I must tell you, I think I could care for.
    They loiter along, eyes lowered decorously,
    But after saying no twice, they'll jump at our company.
FIRST STUDENT. No, no—all that bowing and scraping, it makes
        me feel ill at ease,
    If we don't get a move on we'll lose our two birds in the
        bushes!
    The work-reddened hand that swings the broom Saturdays
    On Sundays knows how to give the softest caresses.
A BURGHER. No, you can have him, our new Mayor,
    Since he took office he's been a dictator, 870
    All he's done is make the town poorer,
    Every day I get madder and madder,
    When he says a thing's so, not a peep, not a murmur
    Dare we express—and the taxes climb higher.
A BEGGAR. [*Singing*]
        Good sirs and all you lovely ladies,
        Healthy in body and handsome in dress,
        Turn, oh turn your eyes on me, please,
        And pity the beggarman's distress!

Must I grind the organ bootlessly?
Only the charitable know true joy.   880
This day when all the world make merry,
Oh make it for me a harvest day.

ANOTHER BURGHER. On a Sunday or holiday nothing in all my
                experience
Beats talking about war and rumors of war,
When leagues away, in Turkey, for instance,
Armies are wading knee deep in gore.
You stand at the window, take long pulls at your schooner,
And watch the gaily colored boats glide past,
And then at sunset go home in the best of humor
And praise God for the blessings of his peace.   890

THIRD BURGHER. Yes, neighbor, yes, exactly my opinion.
Let them go and beat each other's brains in,
Let them turn the whole world upside down,
As long as things are just as always here at home.

OLD CRONE. [*To the Burghers' Daughters*]
Well, aren't we the smart ones! *And* so pretty and young!
I'd like to see the man who could resist you.
But not so proud, my dears! And never fear—I'm mum.
Oh, I know how to get what you want for you.

BURGHER'S DAUGHTER. Agatha, come, we've got to leave!
I'm afraid of being seen with that witchwoman.   900
Oh dear, and only last St. Andrew's Eve
She showed me in a glass my very own one.

HER FRIEND. And mine she showed me in a crystal ball,
Looking a soldier, with cocky friends around him.
And though I seek him everywhere,
It seems that I shall never find him.

SOLDIERS.
Castles have ramparts.
Great walls and towers,
Girls turn their noses up
At soldier-boy lovers—   910
We'll make both ours!

Boldly adventure
And rake in the pay!

Hear the shrill bugle
Summon to battle,
Forward to rapture
Or forward to ruin!
Oh what a struggle!
Our life—oh how stirring!
Haughty girls and great castles,   920
We'll make them surrender!
Boldly adventure
And rake in the pay!
—And after, the soldiers
Go marching away.

    Faust and Wagner.

FAUST. The streams put off their icy mantle
 Under the springtime's kindly smile;
 Hope's green banner flies in the valley;
 White-bearded winter, old and frail,
 Retreats into his mountain fastness,   930
 And still retreating, down he sends
 Feeble volleys of sleet showers,
 Whitening in patches the green plains.
 But the sun can bear with white no longer,
 When life stirs, shaping all anew,
 He wants a scene that has some color,
 And since there's nowhere yet one flower,
 Holiday crowds have got to do.

 Now face about, and looking down
 From the hilltop at the town,   940
 See the many-colored throng
 Passing through the arch of stone
 Into sunshine, out of gloom.
 They celebrate the Resurrection,

For they themselves today are risen:
From airless rooms in huddled houses,
From drudgery at counters and benches,
From under cumbrous roofs and gables,
From crowded, suffocating alleys,
From the mouldering dimness of the churches,   950
All are brought forth into brightness.
And look there, how the eager crowd
Scatters through the fields and gardens,
How over the river's length and breadth
Skiffs and sculls are busily darting,
And that last boat, packed near to sinking,
Already's pulled a good ways off.
Even from distant mountain slopes
Bright colored clothes wink back at us.
Hear all that village noise and confusion?   960
There's where you find the people's real heaven.
Listen to young and old shouting exultingly.
Oh I feel a man here, here's where I should be!

WAGNER. To go for a walk with you, dear Doctor,
Is a treat for my mind as well as honoring me;
But by myself I'd never come here
For I can't abide the least vulgarity.
The screeching fiddles, the shrieking, the playing bowls
For me are all an unbearable uproar,
All scream and shout like possessed souls   970
And call it music, call it pleasure.

PEASANTS. [*Singing and dancing under the linden tree*]
The shepherd dressed up in his best,
Pantaloons and flowered vest,
        Oh my, how brave and handsome!
Within the broad-leaved linden's shade
Madly spun both man and maid,
            Hooray, hooray,
            Hurrah, hurrah, hooray!
        The fiddle bow flew, and then some.

He flung himself into their midst 980
And seized a young thing round the waist,
    While saying, "Care to dance, ma'am?"
The snippy miss she tossed her head,
"You boorish shepherd boy!" she said,
      Hooray, hooray,
      Hurrah, hurrah, hooray!
    "Observe, do, some decorum!"

But round the circle swiftly wheeled,
To right and left the dancers whirled,
    Till all the breath flew from them. 990
They got so red, they got so warm,
They rested, panting, arm in arm,
      Hooray, hooray,
      Hurrah, hurrah, hooray!
    And breast to breast—a twosome.

"I'll thank you not to make so free!
We girls know well how men betray,
    What snakes lurk in their bosom!"
But still he wheedled her away—
Far off they heard the music play, 1000
      Hooray, hooray,
      Hurrah, hurrah, hooray!
    The shouting and the dancing.

OLD PEASANT. Professor, it's so nice of you
    To join us common folk today,
Though such a wise and learned man,
    Not to scorn our holiday.
So please accept our best cup, filled
With good fresh drink. To you I give
It in the hope, not only will 1010
It quench your thirst, but may you live
As many days beyond your lot

As there are drops inside the cup.

FAUST. Friends, thanks for this refreshment, I
In turn wish you all health and joy.
[*The people make a circle around him.*]

OLD PEASANT. Indeed it's only right that you
Should be with us this happy day,
Who when our times were bitter, proved
Himself our friend in every way.
Many a one stands in his boots here   1020
Whom your good father, the last minute,
Snatched from the hot grip of the fever,
That time he quelled the epidemic.
And you yourself, a youngster then,
Never shrank back; every house
The pest went in, you did too.
Out they carried many a corpse,
But never yours. Much you went through;
Us you saved, and God saved you.

ALL. Health to our tried and trusty friend,   1030
And may he help us yet again.

FAUST. Bow down to him who dwells above,
Who is our help, commands us love.
[*He continues on with Wagner.*]

WAGNER. The gratification you must get from all this,
From knowing the reverence these people hold you in!
The man whose gifts can gain him such advantages,
Oh, he's a lucky one in my opinion.
Who is it, each one asks as he rushes up,
Fathers point you out to their boys,
The fiddle stops, the dancers pause,   1040
And as you pass between the rows
Of people, caps fly in the air, why,
Next you know they'll all be on their knees
As if the Host itself were passing by.

FAUST. A few steps more to that rock where we'll rest
A bit, shall we, from our walk. How often

I would sit alone here, plunged in thought,
And torture myself with prayers and with fasting.
So much hope I had then, such firm faith.
I'd wring my hands, I'd weep, fall on my knees,   1050
Believing by these means I could force God
To look down from above and stop the disease.
But now these people's praises seem
A mockery to me. If you could only
See into my heart, you'd understand
How little worthy father and son were really.

  My father was an upright man, a solitary,
Brooding soul who pondered Nature's mysteries
With honest zeal, yet quite fantastically.
Together with other alchemical adepts, he gave   1060
Himself up to the black arts of their kitchen,
Mixing together opposites according
To innumerable recipes. A bold Red Lion,
Handsome suitor he, took for wedding
Partner a pure White Lily, the two uniting
In a tepid bath; then being tested by fire,
The pair precipitately fled
From one bridal chamber to another,
Till there appeared, within the glass,
The young Queen, dazzlingly dressed   1070
In every color of the spectrum:
The Great Specific, Sovereign Medicine.
The patients died; none stopped to inquire
How many there were who had got better.

  So with our infernal electuary
We killed our way across the country.
I poisoned, myself, by prescription, thousands;
They sickened and faded; yet I must live to see
On every side the murderers' fame emblazoned.
WAGNER. But why such violent, such intense emotion?   1080
  When a good man follows, with scrupulous devotion,
The arts his predecessors practised,

He does all that can be expected.
A youth who is respectful of his father
Eagerly soaks up all he has to teach;
If later, thanks to him, our science is enriched,
His son in turn can carry science further.

FAUST. Oh, he's a happy man who hopes
To keep from drowning in these seas of error!
What we know least about, we need the most,   1090
And what we do know, is no use whatever.
   But we mustn't poison with our gloomy thoughts
The sweetness of the present hour!
Look how the sunset's level rays
Gild those cottages in their green bower,
The day fades quietly, the sun departs,
Hurrying off to kindle new life elsewhere—
If only I had wings to bear me up
Into the air and follow after!
Then I would see the whole world at my feet.   1100
Quietly shining in the eternal sunset,
The peaks ablaze, the valleys gone to sleep,
And every silver stream a golden torrent.
The savage mountain with its yawning rifts
Shouldn't ever thwart my godlike soaring,
And there's the ocean, see, already swelling
Before my wondering gaze, with its sun-warmed gulfs.
But finally the bright god looks like sinking,
Whereupon a renewed urgency
Drives me on to drink his eternal light,   1110
The day always before, behind the night,
The heavens overhead, below the heaving sea . . .
   A lovely dream!—and meanwhile it grows dark.
Oh dear, oh dear, that our frames should lack
Wings wherewith to match the spirit's wings.
And yet our nature's such that everybody
Knows feelings that soar upwards, always straining,
When high above, lost in the blue immensity,

The skylark pours out his shrill rhapsody,
When over fir-clad mountain steeps   1120
The eagle on his broad wings gyres slowly,
And passing over prairies, over lakes,
The homeward-bound crane labors steadily.

WAGNER. Well, I've had more than one odd moment, I have,
But I have never felt those impulses you have.
Soon enough you get your fill of woods and things;
I don't really envy birds their wings.
How different are the pleasures of the intellect,
Sustaining one from page to page, from book to book,
And warming winter nights with dear employment   1130
And with the consciousness your life's so lucky.
And goodness, when you spread out an old parchment,
Heaven's fetched straight down into your study.

FAUST. You know the one great driving force,
May you never know the other!
Two souls live in me, alas,
Forever warring with each other.
One, amorous of the world, with all its might
Grapples it close, greedy of all its pleasures;
The other fights to rise out of the dust   1140
Up, up into the heaven of our great forebears.

You beings of the air, if such exist,
Holding sway between the skies and earth,
Come down to me out of the golden haze
And translate me to a new, a vivid life!
Oh, if I only had a magic mantle
To bear me off to unknown lands,
I'd never trade it for the costliest gowns,
Or for a cloak however rich and royal.

WAGNER. Never call down that familiar swarm   1150
That swoops and hovers through the middle air,
Bringing mankind every kind of harm
From every corner of the terrestrial sphere.

Out of the North, sharp-toothed spirits fall
On us and grip us with their chill fingers;
Out of the East, soughing with parched breath,
They suck our lungs dry, shrivel up our innards;
And when from Southern deserts the hot ones
Blow, heaping fire on our heads,
The West ones send for our relief   1160
Rains to cool, then drown, us and our fields.
Their ears are cocked, alert to trip men up;
Seem dutiful because they mean to fool us;
Their pretense is that they are heaven-sent
And lisp like angels even as they cheat us.
    However, come, let's go, the world's turned chill
And dreary, evening mists are rising!
Indoors is where you want to be at nightfall.
But why should you stand still, astonished, staring?
What can you see in the dusk to find upsetting?   1170

FAUST. Don't you see that black dog in the stubble,
    Coursing back and forth?

WAGNER.   I do. I noticed him
    A while back. What about him?

FAUST.   Look again.
    What kind of creature is it?

WAGNER.   Kind? A poodle—
    Who's a nuisance to his master, always
    Searching out his track, the way dogs do.

FAUST.   Look, he's
    Circling around us, coming nearer and nearer.
    Unless I'm much mistaken, a wake of fire
    'S streaming behind him.

WAGNER.   I see nothing
    But a black-haired poodle. Your eyes are playing   1180
    Tricks on you, perhaps.

FAUST.   I think I see
    Him winding a magic snare, quietly,
    Around our feet, a noose which he'll pull tight
    In the future, when the time is ripe.

WAGNER. He's circling us because he's timid and uncertain;
   He's missed his master, come on men unknown to him.
FAUST. The circle's getting tighter, he's much closer!
WAGNER. You see!—a dog and no ghost, sir.
   He growls suspiciously, he hesitates,
   He wags his tail, he sinks down flat—   1190
   Never fear, it's all just dog behavior.
FAUST. Come here, doggie, here, come here!
WAGNER. A silly creature, a poor beast.
   When you stop, he stops too and waits;
   Speak to him, he'll leap and bark;
   Throw something and he'll fetch it back,
   Splash right in the river for your stick.
FAUST. I guess you're right, it's just what he's been taught;
   I see no sign of anything occult.
WAGNER. A dog that's so well-trained, has such good
      manners,   1200
   Why, even a philosopher would like him.
   His student teachers found him an apt scholar—
   Sir, he deserves you should adopt him.
   [*They enter at the City Gate.*]

FAUST'S STUDY [I]

FAUST. [*Entering with the poodle*]
   Behind me lie the fields and meadows
   Underneath the cloak of night,
   With a shuddering sense of premonition
   Our better soul now starts awake.
   Our worser one, unruly, reckless,
   Quietens and starts to nod;
   In me the love of my own fellows   1210
   Begins to stir, and the love of God.

   Poodle, hush! And stop that running!
   What makes you sniff so at the door?

Here's my best cushion for you to doze on
Behind the stove, there on the floor.
Just now when we came down the hillside
We found you an amusing beast;
I'm glad to take you in and feed you,
You're welcome—as a silent guest.

When a man comes back to his cramped little study,   1220
To the friendly lamplight, the coziness,
Oh then it brightens in his bosom
And his heart feels it knows itself.
Again he hears the voice of reason,
And hope revives, it breathes afresh,
He longs to drink the living waters,
Mount upwards to our being's source.

You're growling, poodle! Animal noises
Hardly suit the solemn music
Filling my soul to overflowing.   1230
We're used to people ridiculing
What they hardly understand,
Grumbling at the good and the beautiful—
It makes them so uncomfortable!
Do dogs now emulate mankind?
   Yet even with the best of will
I feel my new contentment fail.
Why must the waters cease so soon
And leave us thirsting once again?
Oh, this has happened much too often!   1240
But there's an answer to it all:
I mean the supernatural,
I mean our hope of revelation,
Which nowhere shines so radiant
As here in the New Testament.
I'll look right now at the original
And see if it is possible

For me to put it, with true feeling,
Into my beloved German.
[*He opens the volume and begins.*]
"In the beginning was the Word"—so goes   1250
The text. And right off I am given pause!
A little help, please, someone! I'm unable
To see the *word* as having supreme value;
If I am filled with the true spirit,
I'll find a better way to say it.
So: "In the beginning, what was?—mind!"
Give plenty of thought to that first line,
Rein in your pen, it's too impetuous:
Is it mind that makes and moves the universe?
Once more: "In vital *force* the world began."   1260
Yet even as I write this sentence down
Something tells me it is still not right.
The spirit speaks, I see the light!
Oh, now I'm sure of it: "First was the act!"

If this cell's one that we'll be sharing,
Poodle, stop that barking, yelping!
You're giving me a splitting headache,
I can't put up with such a roomate.
I'm sorry to say that one of us
Has got to quit the premises.   1270
It goes against the grain with me
To renege on hospitality,
But there's the door, dog, leave, goodbye.

But what the devil's going on?
What I see's beyond belief!
Is it real, is it a phantom?
My poodle's swelled up huger than life!
Now he's rising ponderously;
That isn't any dog, believe me!
What a dreadful spook I've brought   1280

Out of the night into my house!
He looks, with his fierce eyes and jaws,
Just like a hippopotamus.
But I have got you in my power!
With a demi-imp of Hell, as you are,
Solomon's Key is what is called for.

SPIRITS. [*Outside the door*]

There's someone locked up inside there!
Don't dare enter, stay right here!
Like a fox the hunter's snared,
Old Nick trembles, oh he's scared!   1290
But keep a sharp lookout,
Fly this way and that,
Around and about,
And you'll see he's soon out.
If you can help him,
Don't let him sit there,
All of us owe him
For many a favor.

FAUST. Against such a creature, my first defense:
The Spell of the Four Elements.

1300

Let Salamander burn,
Undine wind and turn,
Sylph melt into thin air,
Hobgoblin sweating labor.

Ignorance
Of the elements,
Their powers and properties,
Denies you all mastery
Over the demonry.

Vanish in fire,   1310
Salamander!
Swirl and stream,
Water-child Undine!

Like a meteor burn,
Aërial Sylph!
Grind and churn,
Drudging gnome!
Come out, come out and let's have done!

None of the four
Is in the cur.   1320
Calmly he lies there, grinning at me;
My spells glance off him harmlessly.
—Now hear me conjure
With something stronger.

Are you, grim fellow,
Escaped here from Hell below?
Then look at this symbol
Before which the legions
Of devils and demons
Fearfully bow.   1330

How his hair bristles, how he swells up now!

Creature cast into darkness,
This name then is known to you
Of the never-begotten one,
Wholly ineffable one,
Cruelly pierced in the side one,
Whose blood in the heavens
Is everywhere streaming?

Behind the stove, spellbound, caught,
The demon puffs up gray and bloat,   1340
Expanding into the whole chamber,
Dissolving himself into vapor.
—Now don't you try going through the ceiling!
Down at my feet, do your master's bidding!
You see, my threats are scarcely idle—

Oh I will flush you out, yes, I will!
Don't drag your feet unless you'd like
My triune light to knock you flat!
Don't drag your feet until you force me
To call on my most potent sorcery.   1350

[*The smoke clears, and Mephistopheles, dressed as an itinerant
student, emerges from behind the stove.*]

MEPHISTO. Why all the racket? What's your wish, sir?
FAUST. So you were the one inside the poodle!
    I have to laugh—a wandering scholar!
MEPHISTO. My greetings to you, learned doctor,
    You really had me sweating hard there.
FAUST.
    And what's your name?
MEPHISTO.   Your question's trivial
    From one who finds words superficial,
    Who strives to pass beyond mere seeming
    And penetrate the heart of being.
FAUST. With gentry like yourself, it's common   1360
    To find the name declares what you are
    Very plainly; for example:
    Lord of the Flies, Destroyer, Liar.
    So who are you, I'd like to know?
MEPHISTO. A humble part of that great power
    Which always means evil, always does good.
FAUST. And pray tell what you mean by *that*.
MEPHISTO. I am the spirit that says no, no always!
    And how right I am! For what
    Does everything that comes into existence   1370
    Here on earth deserve, if not
    To be wiped out completely? Much better, surely,
    Nothing ever was. So all that you call sin,
    Catastrophe and ruin—i.e. evil—
    For me's the water I swim in.
FAUST. A part, you say? You look like the whole works to me.

MEPHISTO. I say what's so, it isn't modesty—
    Man in his world of self's a fool,
    He likes to think he's all in all.
    I'm part of the part which was all at first,   1380
    A part of the dark from which light burst forth,
    Arrogant light which now usurps the air
    And seeks to thrust Night from her ancient chair,
    To no avail. Since light is one with all
    Things bodily, making them beautiful,
    Streams from them, from them is reflected,
    Since light by matter's manifested—
    When by degrees all matter's burnt up and no more,
    Why, then light shall not matter any more.
FAUST. Oh, now I understand your office: 1390
    Since you can't wreck things all at once,
    You're going at it by bits and pieces.
MEPHISTO. And making little headway, I confess.
    The opposite of nothing-at-all,
    The *something,* this great shambling world,
    In spite of how I exert myself against it,
    Phlegmatically endures my every onset
    By earthquake, fire, tidal wave and storm:
    Next day the land and sea again are calm.
    And all that *stuff,* those animal and human species—   1400
    I can hardly make a dent in them.
    The numbers I've already buried, armies!
    Yet fresh troops keep on marching up again.
    That's how it is, it's enough to drive you crazy!
    From air, from water, from the earth
    Seeds innumerable sprout forth
    In dry and wet and cold and warm!
    If I hadn't kept back fire for myself,
    What the devil could I call my own?
FAUST. So against the good, the never-resting,   1410
    All-powerful creative force
    In impotent spite you raise your fist and

Try to arrest life's forward thrust.
Look around for work that's more rewarding,
You singular son of old Chaos!

MEPHISTO. Well, it's a subject for discussion—
At our next meeting. Now I wish
To go. That is, with your permission.

FAUST. But why should you ask me for leave?
We've struck up an acquaintance, we two,   1420
Drop in on me whenever you please.
There's the door and there's the window
And your old reliable, the chimney.

MEPHISTO. Well . . . you see . . . an obstacle
Keeps me from dropping *out*—so sorry!
That witch's foot chalked on your doorsill.

FAUST. The pentagram's the difficulty?
But if it's that that has you stopped,
How did you ever manage an entry?
And how should a spirit like you get trapped?   1430

MEPHISTO. Well, look close and you'll see that
A corner's open: the outward pointing
Angle's lines don't quite meet.

FAUST. What a stroke of luck! I'm thinking
Now you are my prisoner.
Pure chance has put you in my power!

MEPHISTO. The poodle dashed right in, saw nothing;
But now the case is the reverse:
The Devil can't get out of the house!

FAUST. There's the window, why don't you use it?   1440

MEPHISTO. It's an iron law we devils can't flout,
The way we come in, we've got to go out,
We're free as to entrée, but not as to exit.

FAUST. So even in Hell there's law and order!
I'm glad, for then a man might sign
A contract with you gentlemen.

MEPHISTO. Whatever we promise, you get, full measure,
There's no cutting corners, no skulduggery—

But it's not a thing to be done in a hurry;
Let's save the subject for our next get-together.   1450
And as for now, I beg you earnestly,
Release me from the spell that binds me!

FAUST. Why rush off, stay a while, do.
I'd love to hear some more from you.

MEPHISTO. Let me go now. I swear I'll come back,
Then you can ask me whatever you like.

FAUST. Don't blame me because you're caught;
You trapped yourself, it's your own fault.
Who's nabbed the Devil must keep a tight grip,
You don't grab him again once he gives you the slip.   1460

MEPHISTO. Oh, all right! To please you I
Will stay and keep you company;
Provided with my arts you let me
Entertain you in my own way.

FAUST. Delighted, go ahead. But please
Make sure those arts of yours amuse!

MEPHISTO. You'll find, my friend, your senses, in one hour,
More teased and roused than all the long dull year.
The songs the fluttering spirits murmur in your ear,
The visions they unfold of sweet desire,   1470
Oh they are more than just tricks meant to fool!
By Arabian scents you'll be delighted,
Your palate tickled, never sated,
The ravishing sensations you will feel!
No preparation's needed, none.
Here we are. Let the show begin!

SPIRITS.

> Open, you gloomy
> Vaulted ceiling above him,
> Let the blue ether
> Look benignly in on him,   1480
> And dark cloudbanks scatter
> So that all is fair for him!
> Small stars are glittering,

Milder suns glowing,
Angelic troops shining
In celestial beauty
Hover past smiling,
Swaying and stooping.
Ardent desire
Follows them yearning;   1490
And their robes streaming ribbons
Veil the fields, veil the meadows,
Veil the arbors where lovers
In pensive surrender
Give themselves to each other
For ever and ever.
Arbor on arbor!
Vines clambering and twining!
Their heavy clusters,
Poured into presses,   1500
Pour out purple wines
Which descend in dark streams
Over beds of bright jewels
Down the vineyards' steep slopes
To broaden to lakes
At the foot of green hills.
Birds blissfully drink there,
With beating wings sunwards soar,
Soar towards the golden isles
Shimmering hazily   1510
On the horizon;
Where we hear voices
Chorusing jubilantly,
Where we see dancers
Whirling exuberantly
Over the meadows,
Here, there and everywhere.
Some climb the heights,

Some swim in the lakes,
Others float in the air—   1520
Joying in life, all,
Beneath the paradisal
Stars glowing with love
Afar in the distance.

MEPHISTO. Asleep! Oh bravely done, my airy younglings!
How duly to his slumbers you have sung him!
I am in your debt for this performance.
—As for you, sir, you were never born
To keep the Prince of Darkness down!
Weave a circle of sweet dreams around him,   1530
Drown him in a deep sea of delusion.
But to break the spell that holds me here,
A rat's tooth is what I require.
No need for conjuring long-windedly—
Listen! I hear a rat rustling already.

The lord of flies and rats and mice,
Of frogs and bedbugs, worms and lice,
Commands you forth from your dark hole
To gnaw, beast, for me that doorsill
Whereon I dab this drop of oil!   1540
—And there you are! Begin, begin!
The corner that is pointing in,
That's the one that shuts me in;
One last crunch to clear my way:
Now Faustus, till we meet next—dream away!

FAUST. [Awakening] Again deceived by tricks, am I?
Do all those vanished spirits only mean:
I saw the Devil in a dream,
Took home a dog that ran away?

FAUST'S STUDY [II]

Faust, Mephistopheles.

FAUST. A knock, was that? Come in! Who is it this time?   1550
MEPHISTO. Me.
FAUST.   Come in!
MEPHISTO.   You have to say it still a third time.
FAUST.

    All right, all right—come in!
MEPHISTO.   Good, very good!
    We two will get along, I see, just as we should.
    I've come here dressed up as a grandee. Why?
    To help you drive your blues away!
    In a scarlet suit, all over gold braid,
    Across my shoulders a stiff silk cape,
    A gay cock's feather in my cap,
    At my side a gallant's long blade—
    And bringing you advice that's short and sweet: 1560
    Put fine clothes on like me, cut loose a bit,
    Be free and easy, man, throw off your yoke
    And find out what real life is like.
FAUST. In any clothes, I'd feel the misery
    Of this cramped, suffocating life on earth.
    I'm too old to live for amusement only,
    Too young to live without desire or wish.
    The world—what has it got to say to me?
    Renounce all that you long for, all—renounce!
    That's the everlasting song-and-dance   1570
    Which you're greeted by on every side,
    The croak you hear year in, year out;
    You can't have what you want, you can't!
    I awake each morning, how? Horrified,
    On the verge of tears, to confront a day
    Which at its close will not have satisfied
    One smallest wish of mine, not one. Why,

Even the hope of a bit of pleasure, some pleasantness,
Withers in the atmosphere of mean-spirited fault-finding;
My eager nature's bold expansiveness   1580
Is brought up short by the daily vexations, jeering.
And when the night draws on and all is hushed,
I go to bed not soothed at last, but apprehensively,
Well knowing what awaits me is not rest,
But wild and whirling dreams that terrify me.
The god who thrones inside my bosom,
Able to shake me to the depths, so powerfully,
The lord and master of my powers,
Is impotent to effect a single thing outside me;
And so I find existence burdensome, wretched,   1590
Death eagerly desired, my life hated.
MEPHISTO. Yet the welcome men give death is never
    wholehearted.
FAUST. Happy the man, even as he conquers gloriously,
    Upon whose brow death sets the blood-stained laurel!
    Happy the man, after dancing the night through furiously,
    Whom it finds out in the white arms of a girl!
    If only, overwhelmed by the Spirit's power,
    In raptures, I had died right then and there!
MEPHISTO. And yet that very night, I seem to remember,
    A fellow didn't down a drink he'd prepared.   1600
FAUST. Spying around, I see, is what you like to do.
MEPHISTO. I don't know everything, but I know a thing or two.
FAUST. If a sweet, familiar strain of music,
    When I was staggering, steadied me,
    Beguiled what's left of childhood feeling
    With echoes of a happier day—
    Well, never again! I pronounce a curse on
    All tales that snare and cheat the soul,
    All false and flattering persuasion
    That ties it to this *corpus vile*.   1610
    First I curse man's mind, for thinking
    Much too well of itself; I curse

The show of things, so dazzling, glittering,
That assails us through our every sense;
Our dreams of fame, of our name's enduring,
Oh what a sham, I curse them too;
I curse as hollow all our having,
Curse wife and child, peasant and plow;
I curse Mammon when he incites us
With dreams of treasure to reckless deeds,   1620
Or plumps the cushions for our pleasure
As we lie lazily at ease;
Curse comfort sucked out of the grape,
Curse love on its pinnacle of bliss,
Curse faith, so false, curse all vain hope,
And patience most of all I curse!

SPIRIT CHORUS. [*Invisible*]

    Oh, what a pity,
    Now you've destroyed it!
    The world once so lovely,
    How you have wrecked it!   1630
    Down it goes, smashed
    By a demigod's fist!
    Out of existence
    We sweep its poor remnants,
    Sorrowing over
    Beauty now lost forever.
    —Then build again, better,
    Potent son of the earth,
    Build a new world, a fairer,
    Inside your own self,   1640
    Within your own heart!
    With a mind clear and strong,
    On your lips a new song,
    Come, make a fresh start!

MEPHISTO. Do you hear them, my angels,
    My dear little wise ones,
    Sagely advising you

To do things, be cheerful?
Their wish is to draw you
Out of the shell you're shut up in,   1650
Out of your torpid stagnation
Into the wide world before you.

Stop making love to your misery,
It gnaws away at you like a vulture;
Even in the meanest company
You'd feel yourself a man like any other.
Not that I'm advising you
To mingle with the multitude;
Among demons I am not a V.I.P.,
But still, if you'll throw in with me,   1660
I'll walk beside you life's long route,
Your good companion. If I suit,
I'm ready to serve you hand and foot.
FAUST. And in return what must I do?
MEPHISTO. There's plenty of time for that, forget it.
FAUST. No, no, the Devil must have his due,
   He doesn't do things for the hell of it,
   Just to see another fellow through.
   So let's hear the terms, what the fine print is;
   Having you for a servant's a tricky business.   1670
MEPHISTO. I promise I will serve your wishes—here,
   A slave who'll do your bidding faithfully;
   But if we meet each other—there,
   Why, you must do the same for me.
FAUST. That "there" of yours—it doesn't scare me off;
   If you pull this world down about my ears,
   Let the other one come on, who cares?
   My joys are part and parcel of this earth,
   It's under this sun that I suffer,
   And once it's goodbye and I've left them   1680
   Then let whatever happens happen,
   And that is that. About the hereafter

We have had enough palaver,
More than I want to hear, by far:
If still we love and hate each other,
If some stand high and some stand lower,
Et cetera, et cetera.

MEPHISTO. In that case, an agreement's easy.
Come, dare it! Come, your signature!
Oh, how my tricks will tickle your fancy!   1690
I'll show you things no man has seen before.

FAUST. You poor devil, really, what have you got to offer?
The mind of man in its sublime endeavor,
Tell me, have you ever understood it?
Oh yes indeed, you've bread: and when I eat it
I'm hungry still; you've yellow gold: like yellow sand
It runs away fast through the hand;
Games of chance no man can win at, ever;
Girls who wind me in their arms, their lover,
While eyeing up a fresh one over my shoulder;   1700
There's honor, that the noblest minds all thirst for:
It shoots across the sky a second, then it's over—
Oh yes, do show me fruit that rots as you try
To pick it, trees whose leaves bud daily, daily die!

[handwritten margin note: all fruit rots / all illusion]

MEPHISTO. Marvels like that? For a devil, not so daunting.
I'm good for whatever you have in mind.
—But friend, the day comes when you find
A share of your own in life's good things,
And peace and quiet, are what you're wanting.

FAUST. If ever you see me loll at ease,   1710
Then it's all yours, you can have it, my life!
If ever you fool me with flatteries
Into feeling satisfied with myself,
Or tempt me with visions of luxuries,
Well, that's my last day on this earth,
I'll bet you!

[handwritten margin note: "sloth..." ↓ acedia— absence of feeling ↓ love]

MEPHISTO.   Done! A Bet!

FAUST.   A bet—agreed!

If ever I plead with the passing moment,
"Linger awhile, oh how lovely you are!"
Then shut me up in close confinement,
I'll gladly breathe the air no more!   1720
Then let the death bell toll my finis,
Then you are free of all your service,
Let the clock wind down, hands fall to pieces,
And time for me be over and done with!

MEPHISTO. Think twice. Forgetting's not a thing we do.

FAUST. Of course, quite right—a bet's a bet.
    This isn't anything I'm rushing into.
    But if I stagnate, fall into a rut,
    I'm a slave, it doesn't matter who to,
    To this one, that one, or to you.   1730

MEPHISTO. My service starts now—no procrastinating!—
    At the dinner tonight for the just-made Ph.D.s.
    But there's one thing: you know, for emergencies,
    I'd like to have our arrangement down in writing.

FAUST. In black and white you want it! Oh, what pedantry!
    You've never learnt a *man's* word's your best surety?
    It's not enough for you that I'm committed
    By what I promise till the end of days?
    —Yet the world's a flood sweeps all along before it,
    And why should I feel my word must hold always?   1740
    A strange idea, but that's the way we are,
    And who would want it otherwise?
    That man's blessed who keeps his conscience clear,
    He'll regret no sacrifice.
    But parchment signed and stamped and sealed,
    Is a bogey all recoil from, scared.
    The pen does in the living word,
    Only sealing wax and vellum count: honor must yield.
    Base spirit, say what you require!
    Brass or marble, parchment or paper?   1750
    Shall I write with quill, with stylus, chisel,
    I leave it up to you, you devil!

MEPHISTO. Why get so hot, make extravagant speeches?

> Ranting away does no good.

> A scrap of paper takes care of the business.

> And sign it with a drop of blood.

FAUST. Oh, all right. If that's what makes you happy,

> I'll go along with the buffoonery.

MEPHISTO. Blood's a very special ink, you know.

FAUST. Are you afraid that I won't keep our bargain?   1760

> Till doomsday I will strive, I'll never slacken!

> So I've promised, that's what I will do.

> I had ideas too big for me,

> Your level's mine, that's all I'm good for.

> The Spirit laughed derisively;

> Nature won't allow me near her.

> Thinking's done with, for ever so long

> Learning and knowledge have sickened me.

> —Then let's unloose our passions, sound

> The depths of sensuality!   1770

> Bring on your miracles, each one,

> Worked by inscrutable sorcery!

> We'll plunge into time's racing current,

> The vortex of activity,

> Where pleasure and distress,

> Setbacks and success,

> May come as they come, by turn-about, however;

> To be always up and doing is man's nature.

MEPHISTO. Go everywhere, sample everything, all sensations,

> And what you like, snatch it up on the run,   1780

> And may they agree with you, all your pleasant diversions!

> Only don't be bashful, wade right in.

FAUST. I told you, I'm not out to enjoy myself, have fun,

> I want frenzied excitements, gratifications that are painful,

> Love and hatred violently mixed,

> Anguish that enlivens, inspiriting trouble.

> Cured of my thirst to know at last,

> I'll never again shun anything distressful;

From now on my wish is to undergo
All that men everywhere undergo, their whole portion,   1790
Make mine their heights and depths, their weal and woe,
Everything human embrace in my single person,
And so enlarge my soul to encompass all humanity,
And shipwreck with them when all shipwreck finally.

MEPHISTO. Believe me, I have chewed away in vain
At that tough meat, mankind, since long ago,
From birth to death's by far too short a time
For any man to digest such a lump of sourdough!
Only a God can take in all of them,
The whole lot. For He dwells in eternal light,   1800
While we poor devils are stuck down below
In darkness and gloom, lacking even candlelight,
And all *you* qualify for is half day, half night.

FAUST. Nevertheless I will!

MEPHISTO.   Bravely proclaimed!
Still, there's one thing worries me.
The time allotted you is very short,
But art has always been around and will be,
So listen, hear what is my thought:
Hire a poet, learn by his instruction.
Let the good gentleman rove through   1810
All the realm of imagination,
And every noble attribute and virtue
He discovers, heap on you, his inspired creation:
  The lion's fierceness,
  Mild hart's swiftness,
  Italian fieriness,
  Northern steadiness.
Let your poet solve that old conundrum,
How to be generous and also cunning;
How, driven by youthful impulsiveness, unrestrained,   1820
To fall in love as beforehand planned.
Such a creature—my, I'd love to know him!—
I'd call him Mr. Microcosm.

FAUST. What am I, then, if it can never be:
  The realization of all human possibility,
  That crown my soul so avidly reaches for?
MEPHISTO. In the end you are—just what you are.
  Wear wigs high-piled with curls, oh millions,
  Stick your legs in yard-high hessians,
  You're still you, the one you always were.   1830
FAUST. I feel it now, how pointless my long grind
  To make mine all the treasures of man's mind;
  When I sit back and interrogate my soul,
  No new powers answer to my call;
  I'm not a hair's breadth more in height,
  A step nearer to the infinite.
MEPHISTO. Dear Dr. Faust, your understanding's
  Ordinary, commonplace;
  We have got the see things better
  Or lose our seat at life's rich feast.   1840
  Hell, man, you have hands and feet,
  A headpiece and a pair of balls;
  And pleasures freshly savored, don't
  You have them too? They're no less yours.
  If I can keep six spanking stallions,
  That horsepower's mine, my property,
  My coach bowls on, ain't I the fellow,
  Two dozen legs I've got for me!
    Sir, come on, quit all that thinking,
  Into the world, the pair of us!   1850
  The man who lives in his head only's
  Like a donkey in the rough
  Led round and round by the bad fairies,
  While green grass grows a stone's throw off.
FAUST. And how do we begin?
MEPHISTO.   By clearing out—just leaving.
  A torture chamber, that's what this place is!
  You call it living, to be boring
  Yourself and your young men to death?

Leave that to Dr. Bacon Fat next door!
Why toil and moil at threshing heaps of straw?   1860
Anyhow, the deepest knowledge you possess
You daren't let on to before your class.
—Oh now I hear one in the passageway!
FAUST. I can't see him—tell him to go away.
MEPHISTO. The poor boy's been so patient, don't be cross;
We mustn't let him leave here *désolé.*
Let's have your cap and gown, Herr Doctor.
Won't I look the fine professor!
[*Changes clothes.*]
Count on me to know just what to say!
Fifteen minutes's all I need for it—   1870
Meanwhile get ready for our little junket!
Exit Faust.

MEPHISTO. [*Wearing Faust's gown*] Despise science, heap
contempt on reason,
The human race's best possession,
Only let the lying spirit draw you
Over into mumbo-jumbo,
Make-believe and pure illusion—
And then you're mine for sure, I have you,
No matter what we just agreed to.
Fate's given him a spirit that's relentless,
It drives him on and on, he can't be stopped,   1880
It soars away beyond all earthly pleasures;
Yet I'll seduce him into roistering about,
Where all proves shallow, meaningless,
Till he is limed and thrashes wildly, stuck;
Before his greedy insatiableness
I'll dangle food and drink; he'll shriek
In vain for relief from his torturing dryness!
And even if he weren't the Devil's already,
He'd still be sure to perish miserably.
[*Enter a student.*]
STUDENT. May I impose, sir, on your kindness?   1890

The object of my visit's to advise with
One whom all the people here
Greatly esteem, indeed revere.

MEPHISTO. I thank you for your courtesy.
But I'm a man, as you can see,
Like any other. Have you perhaps tried elsewhere?

STUDENT. It's you, sir, you, I want for adviser!
I've come here eager and determined,
Anxious to learn whatever's worth learning;
Mother cried to see me go;   1900
I've got an allowance, it's small, but will do.

MEPHISTO. You've come to the right place, my son.

STUDENT. But I'm ready to turn right around and run!
It seems so sad inside these walls,
My heart misgives me; here all's
Confined, shut in; there's nothing green,
Not even a single tree, to be seen.
Oh, I'm unable, in the lecture hall,
To hear or see or think at all!

MEPHISTO. It's a matter of getting used to the place.   1910
At first an infant fights the breast,
But soon it's feeding lustily.
Just so your craving will grow daily
The more you nurse at Wisdom's bosom.

STUDENT. I'll cling tight to her bosom, with pleasure,
But how do I find the way to her?

MEPHISTO. First of all, then—have you chosen
A faculty?

STUDENT.   Well, you see,
I'd like to be a learned man.
The earth below, the heavens on high—   1920
All those things I long to understand,
All the sciences, all nature.

MEPHISTO. You've got the right idea; however,
It demands close application.

STUDENT. Oh never fear, I'm in this heart and soul;

But still, a fellow gets so dull
Without time off for recreation,
In the long and lovely days of summer.

MEPHISTO. Time slips away so fast, you need to use it
Rationally and not abuse it.   1930
And for that reason I advise you:
The Principles of Logic *primo*!
We will drill your mind by rote,
Strap it in the Spanish boot
So it never will forget
The road that's been marked out for it
And stray about incautiously,
A will-o'-the-wisp, this way and that way.
Day after day you'll be taught
All you once did just like that,   1940
Like eating and drinking, thoughtlessly,
Now needs a methodology,
Order and system: *A, B, C!*
  Our thinking instrument behaves
Like a loom: a thousand threads,
At a step on the treadle, are set moving,
Back and forth the shuttles fly,
The strands flow too fast for the eye,
A blow of the batten and there's cloth, woven!
Now enter your philosopher, he   1950
Proves all is just as it should be:
A being thus and *B* also,
Then *C* and *D* inevitably follow;
And if there were no *A* and *B*,
There'd never be a *C* and *D*.
They're struck all of a heap, his admiring hearers,
But still, it doesn't make them weavers.
How do you study something living?
Drive out the spirit, deny it being,
So there're just parts with which to deal,   1960
Gone is that anomalous thing, the soul.

With lifeless pieces as the only things real,
The wonder's where's the life of the whole—
Encheiresis naturae, the chemists then call it,
Make fools of themselves and never know it.
STUDENT. I have trouble following what you say.
MEPHISTO. You'll get the hang of it by and by,
When you learn to distinguish and classify.
STUDENT. How stupid all this makes me feel;
It goes around in my head like a mill.   1970
MEPHISTO. Next, my boy, and let me stress it,
You've got to study metaphysic,
Exert your faculties to venture
Beyond the boundaries of our nature,
Gain intelligence the brain
Has difficulty taking in,
And whether it goes in or not,
There's always a big word for it.
    Your first semester, be very sure
To do things right, attend each lecture.   1980
Five of them you'll have daily;
Be in your seat when the bell peals shrilly.
Come to class with your homework done,
The sections memorized, each one,
So you are sure there's no mistake
And no word's said not in the book.
Still, all your hear set down in your notes
As if it came from the Holy Ghost.
STUDENT. No need to tell me that again,
I realize notes help a lot;   1990
What you've got down in black and white
Goes home with you, is yours for certain.
MEPHISTO. But your faculty—you've still not told me!
STUDENT. Well, I don't think the law would suit me.
MEPHISTO. I can't blame you for disliking it,
Jurisprudence's in a dreadful state,
Laws are like a disease we inherit,

Passed down through generations, spread about
From people to people, place to place;
What once made sense in time becomes nonsensical,   2000
What first was beneficial now's a plague.
O grandsons coming after, how I pity you all!
As for the rights we have from Nature as her heir—
Never a word about *them* will you hear!

STUDENT. I hate the stuff now more than ever!
    How lucky I am to have you for adviser.
    Perhaps I'll take theology.

MEPHISTO. I shouldn't want to lead you astray,
    But it's a science, if you'll allow me to say it,
    Where it's easy to lose your way.   2010
    There's so much poison hidden in it,
    It's very nearly impossible
    To tell what's toxic from what's medicinal.
    Here again it's safer to choose
    One single master and echo his words dutifully—
    As a general rule, put your trust in *words,*
    They'll guide you safely past doubt and dubiety
    Into the Temple of Absolute Certainty.

STUDENT. But shouldn't words convey ideas, a meaning?

MEPHISTO. Of course they should! But why overdo it?   2020
    It's exactly when ideas are lacking
    Words come in so handy as a substitute.
    With words we argue pro and con,
    With words invent a whole system.
    Believe in words! Have faith in them!
    No jot or tittle shall pass from them.

STUDENT. Forgive me, but I have another query.
    It's my last one and then I'll go.
    Medicine, sir—what might you care to tell me
    About that study I should know?   2030
    Three years, my God, is such a short time,
    And the field so broad, it quite defeats me.
    One or two professional suggestions

Helps one along in one's studies wonderfully.
MEPHISTO. [*Aside*] I'm sick of playing the Herr Professor—
Back again to deviltry!
[*Aloud*] Medicine's an easy art to master.
Up and down you study the whole world
Only so as to discover
In the end it's all up to the Lord.   2040
Plough your way through all the sciences you please,
Each learns only what he can;
But the man who understands his opportunities,
Now he's the one I call a man!
You seem a pretty strapping fellow,
Not one to hang back bashfully;
If you don't doubt yourself, I know
Nobody else will doubt you, nobody.
Above all learn your way with women;
Their everlasting sighs and groans,   2050
Their never-ending aches and pains
Have one sole source, there's where to treat them,
And if you don't do things too crudely
You'll have them all just where you want them.
With an M.D. you enjoy great credit,
Your art, they're sure, beats others' arts;
The doctor, when he pays a visit,
For greeting reaches for those parts
It takes a layman years to come at;
You feel her pulse with extra emphasis,   2060
Fix her, slyly, with burning looks,
And slipping your arm around her slender hips,
See if it's because she's so tight-laced.
STUDENT. Oh, that's much better—practical, down to earth!
MEPHISTO. All theory, my dear fellow, is gray,
And green the golden tree of life.
STUDENT. I swear it seems a dream to me!
Would you allow me to impose on
Your generous kindness another day

And drink still more draughts of your wisdom?   2070

MEPHISTO. I'm glad to help you in whatever way.

STUDENT. I mustn't leave without presenting

     You my album. Do write something

     In it for me, would you?

MEPHISTO.   Gladly.

           [*Writes and hands back the album.*]

STUDENT. [*Reading*] *Eritis sicut Deus, scientes bonum et malum.*

           [*Closes the book reverently and exits.*]

MEPHISTO. Faithfully follow that good old verse,

     That favorite line of my aunt's, the snake,

     And for all your precious godlikeness,

     You'll end up how? A nervous wreck.

           Enter Faust.

FAUST. And now where to?

MEPHISTO.   Wherever you like.   2080

     First we'll mix with little people, then with great.

     The pleasure and the profit you will get

     From our course—and never pay tuition for it!

FAUST. But me and my long beard—we're hardly suited

     For the fast life. I feel myself defeated

     Even before we start. I've never been

     A fellow to fit in. Among other men

     I feel so small, so mortified, so fazed.

     Oh, in the world I'm always ill at ease!

MEPHISTO. My friend, that's all soon changed, it doesn't

           matter;   2090

     With confidence comes *savoir-vivre.*

FAUST. But how do we get out of here?

     Where are your horses, groom and carriage?

MEPHISTO. The way we're going is by air,

     Upon my cloak—you'll enjoy the voyage.

     But take care, on so bold a tour,

     You're sparing in the matter of luggage.

     I'll heat some gas, that way we'll lift

     Quickly off the face of earth;

If we're light enough we'll rise right up—   2100
Congratulations, sir, on your new life!

AUERBACH'S CELLAR IN LEIPZIG

Drinker's Carousing.

FROSCH. Faces glum and glasses empty?
    I don't call this much of a party.
    You fellows seem wet straw tonight,
    Who always used to blaze so bright.
BRANDER. It's your fault—he just sits there, hardly speaks!
    Where's the horseplay, where're the dirty jokes?
FROSCH. [*Emptying a glass of wine on his head*]
    There! Both at once!
BRANDER.   O horse and swine!
FROSCH. You asked for it, so don't complain.
SIEBEL. Out in the street if you want to punch noses!   2110
    —Now take a deep breath and roar out a chorus
    In praise of the grape and the jolly god Bacchus.
    Come, all together with a rollicking round-o!
ALTMAYER. Stop, stop, man, I'm wounded, someone fetch me
        some cotton,
    The terrible fellow has burst me an eardrum!
SIEBEL. Hear the sound rumble above in the vault?
    That tells you you're hearing the true bass note.
FROSCH. That's right! Out the door, whoever don't like it!
    With a do-re-mi,
ALTMAYER. And a la-ti-do,   2120
FROSCH. We will have us a concert!
    [*Sings.*]
        Our dear Holy Roman Empire.
        How does the damn thing hold together?
BRANDER. Oh, but that's awful, a terrible tune!
    A dreary, disgusting *political* song!

Thank the Lord when you wake each morning
You're not the one must keep the Empire going.
It's a blessing I'm grateful for
To be neither Kaiser nor Chancellor.
But we, too, need a chief for our group,   2130
So let's elect ourselves a pope.
To all of us here I'm sure it's well known
What a man must do to sit on that throne.

FROSCH. [*Singing*]
　　Nightingale, fly away, o'er lawn, o'er bower,
　　Tell her I love her ten thousand times over.

SIEBEL. Enough of that love stuff, it turns my stomach.

FROSCH. Ten thousand times, though it drives you frantic!
　[*Sings.*]
　　Unbar the door, the night is dark!
　　Unbar the door, my love, awake!
　　Bar up the door now it's daybreak.   2140

SIEBEL. Go on, then, boast about her charms, her favor,
But I will have the latest laugh of all.
She played me false—just wait, she'll play you falser.
A horned imp's what I wish her, straight from Hell,
To dawdle with her in the dust of crossroads;
And may an old goat stinking from the Brocken
Bleat "Goodnight, dearie," to her, galloping homewards.
A fellow made of honest flesh and blood
For a slut like that is much too good.
I know the way I'd send my love to her—and how!   2150
With a rock heaved through her kitchen window.

BRANDER. [*Banging on the table*]
Good fellows, your attention! None here will deny
I know what should be done and shouldn't at all.
Now we have lovers in our company
Whom we must treat in manner suitable
To their condition, our jollity,
With a song just lately written. So mind the air
And come in on the chorus loud and clear!

[*He sings.*]

A rat lived downstairs in the cellar,
Dined every day on lard and butter,   2160
His paunch grew round as any burgher's,
As round as Dr. Martin Luther's.
The cook put poison down for it,
Oh, how it groaned, the pangs it felt,
    As if by Cupid smitten.

CHORUS. [*Loud and clear*]
    As if by Cupid smitten!

BRANDER.

It rushed upstairs, it raced outdoors
And drank from every gutter,
It gnawed the woodwork, scratched the floors,
Its fever burned still hotter,   2170
In agony it hopped and leaped,
Oh, piteously the creature squeaked,
    As if by Cupid smitten.

CHORUS.
    As if by Cupid smitten!

BRANDER.

Its torment drove it, in broad day,
Out into the kitchen;
Collapsing on the hearth, it lay
Panting hard and twitching.
But that cruel Borgia only laughed:
Ha, ha, the brute's at its last gasp,   2180
    As if by Cupid smitten.

CHORUS.
    As if by Cupid smitten!

SIEBEL. You find it funny, you coarse louts,
    Oh, quite a stunt, so very cunning,
    To put down poison for poor rats!
BRANDER. You feel for them, you find them touching?
ALTMAYER. O big of gut and bald of pate!
    Losing out's subdued the oaf;

What he sees in the bloated rat
'S the spitting image of himself.   2190
    [*Faust and Mephistopheles enter.*]
MEPHISTO. What your case calls for, Doctor, first,
  Is some amusing company,
  To teach you life can be so easy.
  For these men every night's a bout
  And every day a holiday;
  With little wit but lots of noise,
  All spin inside their little orbit
  Like young cats chasing their own tails.
  As long as the landlord grants them credit
  And they are spared a splitting headache,   2200
  They're satisfied and have no cares.
BRANDER. They're travelers, come here from elsewhere,
  You can tell it by their foreign manner—
  They've not been here, I'll bet, an hour.
FROSCH. Right, right! My Leipzig's an attraction, how I love her,
  A little Paris spreading light and culture!
SIEBEL. Who might they be? What's your guess?
FROSCH. Leave it to me. I'll fill their glass,
  Gently extract, as you do a baby's tooth,
  All there is to know about them, the whole truth.   2210
  I'd say we're dealing with nobility,
  They look so proud, so dissatisfied, to me.
BRANDER. They're pitchmen at the Fair, is what I think.
ALTMAYER. Maybe.
FROSH.   Now watch me go to work.
MEPHISTO. [*To Faust*]
  These dolts can't ever recognize Old Nick
  Even when he's got them by the neck.
FAUST. Gentlemen, good day.
SIEBEL.   Thank you, the same.
  [*Aside, obliquely studying Mephistopheles*]
  What the hell, the fellow limps, he's lame!
MEPHISTO. We'd like to join you, sirs, if you'll allow it.

About my landlord's wine I don't feel sanguine,   2220
So the company shall make up for it.

ALTMAYER. Particular, you are, about your drinking.

FROSCH. Fresh from Dogpatch, right? From supper
On cabbage soup with Goodman Clodhopper?

MEPHISTO. We couldn't stop on this trip, more's the pity!
But last time he went on so tenderly
About his Leipzig kith and kin,
And sent his very best to you, each one.

Bowing to Frosch.

ALTMAYER. [*Aside to Frosch*]
Score one for him. He's got some wit.

SIEBEL. A sly one, he is.

FROSCH.   Wait, I'll fix him yet!   2230

MEPHISTO. Unless I err, weren't we just now hearing
Some well-schooled voices joined in choral singing?
Voices, I am sure, must resonate
Inside this vault to very fine effect.

FROSCH. You know music professionally, I think.

MEPHISTO. Oh no—the spirit's eager, but the voice is weak.

ALTMAYER. Give us a song!

MEPHISTO.   Whatever you'd like to hear.

SIEBEL. A new one, nothing we ever heard before.

MEPHISTO. Easily done. We've just come back from Spain,
Land where the air breathes song, the rivers run wine.   2240
[*Sings.*]
Once upon a time a King
Had a flea, a big one—

FROSCH. Did you hear that? A flea, goddamn!
I'm all for fleas, myself, I am.

MEPHISTO. [*Sings*]
Once upon a time a King
Had a flea, a big one,
Doted fondly on the thing
With fatherly affection.
Calling his tailor in, he said,

Fetch needles, thread and scissors,   2250
   Measure the Baron up for shirts,
   Measure him, too, for trousers.
BRANDER. And make it perfectly clear to the tailor
   He must measure exactly, sew perfect stitches,
   If he's fond of his head, not the least little error,
   Not a wrinkle, you hear, not one, in those breeches!
MEPHISTO.
   Glowing satins, gleaming silks
      Now were the flea's attire,
   Upon his chest red ribbons crossed
      And a great star shone like fire,   2260
   In sign of his exalted post
      As the King's First Minister.
   His sisters, cousins, uncles, aunts
      Enjoyed great influence too—
   The bitter torments that that Court's
      Nobility went through!
   And the Queen as well, and her lady's maid,
      Though bitten till delirious,
   Forbore to squash the fleas, afraid
      To incur the royal animus.   2270
   But we free souls, we squash all fleas
      The instant they light on us!
CHORUS. [*Loud and clear*]
   But we free souls, we squash all fleas
      The instant they light on us!
FROSCH. Bravo, bravo! That was fine!
SIEBEL. May every flea's fate be the same!
BRANDER. Between finger and nail, then crack! and they're
   done for.
ALTMAYER. Long live freedom, long live wine!
MEPHISTO. I'd gladly drink a glass in freedom's honor,
   If only your wine was a little better.   2280
SIEBEL. Talk like that around here isn't popular!
MEPHISTO. I'm sure our landlord wouldn't take it kindly,

Otherwise I'd treat this company
To wine that's wine—straight out of our own cellar.
SIEBEL. Go on, go on, let the landlord be my worry.
FROSCH. You're princes, you are, if you're able
    To put good wine upon the table;
    But a drop or two, well, that's no trial at all,
    To judge right what I need's a real mouthful.
ALTMAYER. [*In an undertone*] They're from the Rhineland,
    I would swear.   2290
MEPHISTO. Let's have an auger, please.
BRANDER.   What for?
    Don't tell me you've barrels piled outside the door!
ALTMAYER. There's a basket of tools—look, over there.
MEPHISTO. [*Picking out an auger, to Frosch*]
    Now gentlemen, name what you'll have, please.
FROSCH. What do you mean? We have a choice?
MEPHISTO. Whatever you wish, I will produce.
ALTMAYER. [*To Frosch*] Licking his lips already, he is!
FROSCH. Fine, fine! For me—a Rhine wine any day,
    The best stuff's from the Fatherland, I say.
MEPHISTO. [*Boring a hole in the table edge at Frosch's place*]
    Some wax to stop the holes with, quick!   2300
ALTMAYER. Hell, it's just a sideshow trick.
MEPHISTO. [*To Brander*]
    And you?
BRANDER. ·   The best champagne you have, friend, please,
    With lots of sparkle, lots of fizz.

[*Mephistopheles goes round the table boring holes at all the places,
which one of the drinkers stops with bungs made of wax.*]

    You can't always avoid what's foreign;
    About pleasure I'm nonpartisan.
    A man who's a true German can't stand Frenchmen,
    But he can stand their wine, oh how he can!
SIEBEL. [*As Mephistopheles reaches his place*]
    I confess your dry wines don't

Please my palate, I'll take sweet.

MEPHISTO. Tokay for you! Coming up shortly!   2310

ALTMAYER. No, gentlemen! Look at me honestly,
    The whole thing's meant to make fools of us.

MEPHISTO. Come on, my friend, I'm not so obtuse!
    Trying something like that on you would be risky.
    So what's your pleasure, I'm waiting—speak!

ALTMAYER. Whatever you like, just don't take all week.

MEPHISTO. [*All the holes are now bored and stopped; gesturing*
    grotesquely]
    Grapes grow on the vine,
    Horns on the head of the goat,
    O vinestock of hard wood,
    O juice of the tender grape!   2320
    And a wooden table shall,
    When summoned, yield wine as well!
    O depths of Nature, mysterious, secret,
    Here is a miracle—if you believe it!
    Now pull the plugs, all, drink and be merry!

ALL. [*Drawing the bungs and the wine each drinker asked for*
    gushing into his glass]
    Sweet fountain, flowing for us only!

MEPHISTO. But take good care you don't spill any.
    [*They drink glass after glass.*]

ALL. [*Singing*]
    How lovely everything is, I'm dreaming!
    Like cannibals having a feast,
    Like pigs in a pen full of slops!   2330

MEPHISTO. They feel so free, what a time they're having!

FAUST. I'd like to depart now. Might we, perhaps?

MEPHISTO. Before we do, you must admire
    Their swinishness in its full splendor.

SIEBEL. [*Spilling wine on the floor, where it bursts into flame*]
    All Hell's afire, I burn, I burn!

MEPHISTO. [*Conjuring the flame*]
    Peace, my own element, down, down!

[*To the drinkers*]

Only a pinch, for the present, of the purgatorial fire.

SIEBEL. What's going on here? For this you'll pay dear!

You don't seem to know the kind of men you have here.

FROSCH. Once is enough for that kind of business!   2340

ALTMAYER. Throw him out on his ear, but quietly, no fuss!

SIEBEL. You've got your nerve, trying out on us

Stuff like that—damned hocus-pocus!

MEPHISTO. Quiet, you tub of guts!

SIEBEL.   Bean pole, you!

Now he insults us. I know what to do.

BRANDER. A taste of our fists is what: one-two, one-two.

ALTMAYER. [*Drawing a bung and flames shooting out at him*]

I'm on fire, I'm on fire!

SIEBEL.   It's witchcraft, no mistaking!

Stick him, the rogue, he's free for the taking!

[*They draw their knives and fall on Mephistopheles.*]

MEPHISTO. [*Gesturing solemnly*]

    False words, false shapes

    Addle wits, muddle senses!   2350

    Let here and otherwheres

    Change their places!

[*All stand astonished and gape at each other.*]

ALTMAYER. Where am I? What a lovely country!

FROSCH. Such vineyards! Do my eyes deceive me?

SIEBEL. And grapes you only need to reach for!

BRANDER. Just look inside this green arbor!

What vines, what grapes! Cluster on cluster!

[*He seizes Siebel by the nose. The others do the same to each other, and raise their knives.*]

MEPHISTO. Unspell, illusion, eyes and ears!

    —Take note the Devil's a jester, my dears!

[*He vanishes with Faust; the drinkers recoil from each other.*]

SIEBEL. What's happened?

ALTMAYER.   What?

FROSCH.   Was that your nose?   2360

BRANDER. [*To Siebel*] And I'm still holding on to yours!
ALTMAYER. The shock I felt—in every limb!
    Get me a chair, I'm caving in.
FROSCH. But what the devil was it, tell me.
SIEBEL. If I ever catch that scoundrel,
    He won't go home alive, believe me!
ALTMAYER. I saw him, horsed upon a barrel,
    Vault straight out through the cellar door—
    My feet feel leaden, so unnatural.
    [*Turning toward the table.*]
    Well—maybe some wine's still trickling there.   2370
SIEBEL. The whole thing was a fraud, a gyp.
FROSCH. I was drinking wine, I'd swear.
BRANDER. And all those grapes—I can tell a grape!
ALTMAYER. Now try and tell me, you know-it-alls,
    There's no such thing as miracles!

WITCH'S KITCHEN

A low hearth, and on the fire a large cauldron. In the steam rising up from it, various figures can be glimpsed. A she-ape is seated by the cauldron, skimming it to keep it from boiling over. The male with their young crouches close by, warming himself. Hanging on the walls and from the ceiling are all sorts of strange objects, the household gear of a witch.

Faust, Mephistopheles.

FAUST. Why, it's revolting, all this crazy witchery!
    Are you telling me I'll learn to be a new man
    Stumbling around in this lunatic confusion?
    Is an ancient hag the doctor who will cure me?
    And that stuff that beast's stirring, that's the remedy   2380
    To cancel thirty years, unbow my back?
    If you can do no better, the outlook's black
    For me, the hopes I nursed are dead already.

Hasn't the mind of man, instructed by Nature,
Discovered some sort of balm, some potent elixer?

MEPHISTO. Now you're speaking sensibly!
There *is* a natural way to recover your youth;
But that's another business entirely
And not your sort of thing, is my belief.

FAUST. No, no, come on, I want to hear it.   2390

MEPHISTO. All right. It's simple: you don't need to worry
About money, doctors, necromancy.
Go out into the fields right now, this minute,
Start digging and hoeing away, working the land,
Confine yourself and your thoughts to the narrowest sphere,
Eat nothing but the plainest kind of fare,
Live with the cattle as cattle, don't feel ashamed
To spread dung on the ground with your own hand.
So there you have it, the sane way, the healthy,
To keep yourself young till the age of eighty!   2400

FAUST. Yes, not my sort of thing, I'm afraid,
Humbling myself to work with a spade;
So straitened a life would never suit me.

MEPHISTO. So it's back to the witch, my friend, are we?

FAUST. That horrible hag—no one else will do?
Why can't *you* concoct the brew?

MEPHISTO. A nice thing that would be, to waste the time of the
Devil
When his every moment is claimed by the business of evil!
Please understand. Not only skill and science
Are called for here, but also patience: 2410
A mind must keep at it for years, very quietly,
Only time can supply the mixture its potency.
Such a deal of stuff goes into the process,
All very strange, mysterious!
The Devil, it's true, taught her how to do it,
But it's no business of his to brew it.
[*Seeing the apes*]
See here, those creatures, aren't they pretty!

That one's the housemaid, that one's the flunkey.

[*To the apes*]

Madam is not at home, it seems?

APES.

  Flew straight up the chimney   2420

  To dine out with friends.

MEPHISTO. And her feasting, how long does it usually take her?

APES. As long as we warm our paws by the fire.

MEPHISTO. [*To Faust*] What do you think of this elegant troupe?

FAUST. Nauseating—make me want to throw up.

MEPHISTO. Well, just this sort of causerie

  Is what I find most entertains me.

  [*To the apes*]

  Tell me, you ugly things, oh do,

  What's that you're stirring there, that brew?

APES. Beggars' soup, it's thin stuff, goes down easy.   2430

MEPHISTO. Your public's assured—they like what's wishy-washy.

HE-APE. [*Sidling up to Mephistopheles fawningly*]

  Oh let the dice roll,

  I need money, and quick,

  Let me win, make me rich,

  I'm so down on my luck.

  With a purse full of thaler,

  An ape passes for clever.

MEPHISTO. How very happy that monkey would be

  If he could buy chances in the lottery.

[*Meanwhile the young apes have been rolling around a big ball to which they now give a push forward.*]

HE-APE.

  The world, sirs, behold it!   2440

  The up side goes down,

  The down side goes up,

  And there's never a respite.

  Touch it, it'll ring,

  It's like glass, fractures easily.

When all's said and done,
A hollow, void thing.
Here it shines brightly,
And brighter here—tinsel!
—Oops, ain't I nimble!   2450
But you, son, take care
And keep a safe distance,
Or surely you'll die.
The thing's made of clay,
A knock, and it's fragments.

MEPHISTO. What is that sieve for?

HE-APE. [*Taking it down*]
If you came here to thieve,
It would be my informer.

[*He scampers across to the she-ape and has her look through it.*]
Look through the sieve!
Now say, do you know him?   2460
Or you don't dare to name him?

MEPHISTO. [*Approaching the fire*] And this pot over here?

APES.
Oh, you're a blockhead, sir—
Don't know what a pot's for!
Nor a cauldron neither.

MEPHISTO. What a rude creature!

HE-APE.
Here, take this duster,
Sit down in the armchair.

[*Presses Mephistopheles down in the chair.*]

FAUST. [*Who meanwhile has been standing in front of a mirror,
        going forward to peer into it from close up and then
        stepping back*]
What do I see? It's a magic mirror!
What a vision of beauty! Love lend me your pinions,   2470
The swiftest you have, so I may speed to her,
Love, show me the way to the heaven she dwells in!
Oh dear, unless I stay fixed to this spot,

If I dare to move the least bit nearer,
Mist blurs the vision and quite obscures her.
Woman unrivaled, beauty absolute!
Can such things be, a creature so lovely?
The body so indolently stretched out there
Surely epitomizes all that is heavenly.
Can such a marvel inhabit down here?   2480
MEPHISTO. Naturally, if God has sweated hard for six whole days,
And on the seventh himself cries Bravo! seeing his works,
You can be sure he's obtained better than average results.
Look all you want now, stare away, gaze;
But I can put your hands on that prize,
And happy the man, his fortune's assured,
Who can bring home such a sweetie to his bed and board.

[*Faust continues to stare into the mirror, while Mephistopheles,
leaning back comfortably in the armchair and toying with the feather
duster, talks on.*]

Here I sit like a king on a throne,
Scepter in hand, all I'm lacking's my crown.
APES. [*Who have been performing all sorts of queer, involved
        movements, with loud cries bring Mephistopheles a crown*]
        Here, your majesty,   2490
        If you would,
        Glue up the crown
        With sweat and blood!

[*Their clumsy handling of the crown causes it to break in two, and
they cavort around with the pieces.*]

        Oh there, now it's broken!
        We look and we listen,
        We chatter, scream curses,
        And make up our verses—
FAUST. [*Still gazing raptly into the mirror*]
        Good God, how my mind reels, it's going to snap!
MEPHISTO. [*Nodding toward the apes*]

My own head's starting to spin like a top.

APES.

>   And if by some fluke   2500
>   The words happen to suit
>   Then the rhyme makes a thought!

FAUST. [*As above*] I feel as if my insides are on fire!

Come, we've got to get out of here.

MEPHISTO. [*Keeping his seat*] They tell the truth, these poets do,

You've got to give the creatures their due.

[*The cauldron, neglected by the she-ape, starts to boil over, causing a great tongue of flame to shoot up the chimney. The Witch comes riding down the flame, shrieking hideously.*]

THE WITCH. It hurts, it hurts!

Monkeys, apes, incompetent brutes!

Forgetting the pot and singeing your mistress—

The servants I have! Utterly brainless!   2510

[*Catching sight of Faust and Mephistopheles*]

>   What's this? What's this?
>   Who are you? Explain!
>   What's your business?
>   Sneaking your way in!
>   Hellfire's pains
>   Torture your bones!

[*She plunges the spoon into the cauldron and scatters fire over Faust, Mephistopheles and the apes. The apes whine.*]

MEPHISTOPHELES. [*Turning the duster upside down and hitting out violently among the glasses and jars with the butt end*]

>   Let's knock things around,
>   Let's have a good smashup!
>   It's all in fun, really—
>   Beating time, you old carcass,   2520
>   To your melody.

[*The witch starts back in rage and fear.*]

Can't recognize me, can you, rattlebones?

Can't recognize your lord and master?
Why I don't chop up you and your monkey friends
Into the littlest bits and pieces is a wonder!
No respect at all for my red doublet?
And my cock's feather means nothing to you, beldam?
Is my face masked, or can you plainly see it?
Must I tell *you* of all people who I am?

THE WITCH. Oh sir, forgive my discourteous salute!   2530
But I look in vain for your cloven foot,
And your two ravens, where are they?

MEPHISTO. Well, this time you're let off—I remember,
It's been so long since we've seen each other.
Also, the world's grown so cultured today,
Even the Devil's been swept up in it;
The northern bogey has made his departure,
No horns now, no tail, to make people shiver;
And as for my hoof, though I can't do without it,
Socially it would raise too many eyebrows,   2540
And so, like a lot of other young fellows,
I've padded my calves to try and conceal it.

THE WITCH. [*Dancing with glee*]
I'm out of my mind with delight, I am,
My lord Satan's appeared again.

MEPHISTO. Woman, that name—I forbid you to speak it!

THE WITCH. Why not? Whatever's wrong with it?

MEPHISTO. Since God knows when, it belongs to mythology,
But that's hardly improved the temper of humanity.
The Evil One's no more, evil ones more than ever.
Address me as Baron, that will do,   2550
A gentleman of rank like any other.
And if you doubt my blood is blue,
See, here's my house's arms, the noblest ever!
[*He makes an indecent gesture.*]

THE WITCH. [*Laughing excessively*]
Ha, ha! It's you, it's you, I swear,
The same old rascal you always were!

MEPHISTO. [*To Faust*] Observe, friend, my diplomacy
    And learn the art of witch-mastery.

THE WITCH. Gentlemen, now what's your pleasure?

MEPHISTO. A generous glass of your famous liquor.
    But please, let it be from your oldest stock: 2560
    It doubles in strength as the years mount up.

THE WITCH. At once! Here I've got, as it happens, a bottle
    From which I myself every now and then tipple,
    And what is more, it's lost all its stink.
    I'll gladly pour you out a cup.
    [*Under her breath*]
    But if the fellow's unprepared, the drink
    Might kill him, you know, before an hour's up.

MEPHISTO. I know the man well, he'll thrive on it;
    I wish him the best your kitchen affords.
    Now draw your circle, say the magic words,   2570
    And pour him out a brimming goblet.

[*Making bizarre gestures, the witch draws a circle and sets down
an assortment of strange objects inside it. All the glasses start to ring
and the pots to resound, providing a kind of musical accompaniment.
Last of all, she brings out a great tome and stands the apes in the circle
to serve as a lectern and to hold up the torches. Then she signals Faust
to approach.*]

FAUST. [*To Mephistopheles*]
    What's to be hoped from this, would you tell me?
    That junk of hers, and her waving her arms crazily,
    All the crude deceptions she's practicing—
    I know them too well, they fill me with loathing.

MEPHISTO. Nonsense, friend, it's not all that serious;
    Really, you're being much too difficult.
    She needs a bit of hocus-pocus
    For her elixer to produce a result.
    [*He presses Faust inside the circle.*]

THE WITCH. [*Declaiming from the book, with great emphasis*]

Hearken to me!   2580
From one make ten,
Now two goes in,
And after, a three,
And lo, you are rich!
Drop the four!
From five and six,
So says the witch,
Make seven and eight,
And all's complete.
And nine is one,   2590
And ten is none,
And now my witch's table's done.

FAUST. I think the old woman's throwing a fit.

MEPHISTO. We're nowhere near the end of it.
    I know the book, it's all like that.
    The time I've wasted over it!
    For a thoroughgoing paradox is what
    Bemuses fools and wise men equally.
    The trick's got a beard, yet it's still going strong:
    With Three-in-One and One-in-Three   2600
    Lies are sown broadcast, truth may go hang.
    The Doctor drones on in undisturbed peace:
    Who wants to debate and dispute with a fool?
    People dutifully think, hearing all that glib speech,
    It can't be such big words mean nothing at all.

THE WITCH. [*Continuing*]
    The power of wisdom
    From the whole world kept hidden
    Save from those who don't think—
    To them it is given
    Unsought and unbidden,   2610
    It's theirs without sweat.

FAUST. Did you hear that, my God, what nonsense,
    It's giving me a headache, phew!

It makes me think I'm listening to
A hundred thousand fools in chorus.
MEPHISTO. Enough, enough, O excellent Sibyl!
    Bring on the potion, fill the cup.
    Your drink won't give my friend here trouble,
    He's earned his Ph.D. in many a bout.

[*The Witch very ceremoniously pours the potion into a bowl; when
Faust raises it to his lips, a low flame plays over it.*]

    Drink, now drink, no need to diddle,   2620
    It'll put you into a fine glow.
    When you've got a sidekick in the Devil,
    Why should some fire frighten you so?
    [*The Witch breaks the circle and Faust steps out.*]
    Now let's be off, you mustn't dally.
THE WITCH. I hope that little nip, sir, hits the spot!
MEPHISTO. [*To the Witch*] Madam, thanks. If I can help *you* out,
    Don't fail, upon Walpurgis Night, to ask me.
THE WITCH. [*To Faust*] Here is a song, sir, carol it now and then,
    You'll find it assists the medicine.
MEPHISTO. Come away quick! You must do as I say.   2630
    To soak up the potion body and soul,
    A man's got to sweat a bucketful.
    And after, I'll teach you the gentleman's way
    Of wasting your time expensively.
    Soon yours the delight outdelights all things—
    Boy Cupid astir in you, stretching his wings.
FAUST. A last look in the mirror, let me—
    That woman was so very lovely!
MEPHISTO. No, no, soon enough you'll behold in the flesh
    The fairest woman that ever drew breath.   2640
    [*Aside*] With that stuff in him, old Jack will
    Soon see a Helen in every Jill.

A STREET

Faust. Margarete passing by.

FAUST. Pretty lady, here's my arm,
    Would you allow me to see you home?
MARGARETE. I'm neither pretty nor a lady,
    And I can find my way unaided.
    [*She escapes his arm and passes by.*]
FAUST. By God, what a lovely girl,
    I've never seen her like, a pearl!
    A good girl, too, and quick-witted,
    Her behavior modest and yet spirited,   2650
    Those glowing cheeks, lips like a rose,
    Will haunt me till the end of days!
    The way she looked down shamefastly
    Touched me to the heart, profoundly;
    And bringing me up short, quite speechless—
    Oh that was charming, that was priceless!
                    Enter Mephistopheles.
FAUST. Get me that girl, do you hear, you must!
MEPHISTO. What girl?
FAUST.   The one who just went past.
MEPHISTO. Oh, her. She's just been to confession
    To be absolved of all her sins.   2660
    I sidled near the box to listen:
    She could have spared herself her pains,
    She is the soul of innocence
    And has no reason, none at all,
    To visit the confessional.
    Her kind is too much for me.
FAUST. She's over fourteen, isn't she?
MEPHISTO. Well, listen to him, the lady-killer,
    Eager to pluck every flower he sees,
    Who's quite convinced that every favor   2670
    Is his to have, hand it over, please.

But it doesn't go so easy always.

FAUST.   Dear Doctor of What's Right and Proper,
  Spare me your lectures, I can do without.
  Let me tell you it straight out:
  If I don't hold that darling creature
  Tight in my arms this very night,
  We're through, we two, at stroke of midnight.

MEPHISTO.   Impossible! That's out of the question!
  I must have two weeks at least   2680
  To spy out a propitious occasion.

FAUST.   With a quiet hour or so, at the most,
  I could seduce her handily—
  Don't need the Devil to pimp for me.

MEPHISTO.   You're talking like a Frenchman now.
  Calm down, there's no cause for vexation.
  You'll find that instant gratification
  Disappoints; if you allow
  For compliments and billets doux,
  Whisperings and rendezvous,   2690
  The pleasure's felt so much more keenly.
  Italian novels teach you exactly.

FAUST.   I've no use for your slow-paced courting;
  My appetite needs no whetting.

MEPHISTO.   Please, I'm being serious.
  With such a pretty little miss
  You mustn't be impetuous
  And assault the fortress frontally.
  What's called for here is strategy.

FAUST.   Something of hers, do you hear, I require! 2700
  Come, show me the way to the room she sleeps in,
  Get me a scarf, a glove, a ribbon,
  A garter with which to feed my desire!

MEPHISTO.   To prove to you my earnest intention
  By every means to further your passion,
  Not losing a minute, without delay
  I'll take you to her room today.

FAUST. I'll see her, yes? And have her?

MEPHISTO. No!

    She'll be at a neighbor's—you *must* go slow!

    Meanwhile in her room, alone there, 2710

    You can drink her atmosphere

    And dream of the delights to come.

FAUST. Can we start now?

MEPHISTO. Too soon, too soon!

FAUST. Well, find me a present I can give her.

Exit.

MEPHISTO. Presents already? The man's proving a lover!

    Now for his gift. I know there's treasure

    Buried in many an out-of-the-way corner.

    Off I go to reconnoiter!

EVENING

A small room, very neat and clean.

MARGARETE. [*As she braids her hair and puts it up*]

    Who was he, I wonder, that gentleman,

    Who spoke to me this afternoon? 2720

    I wish I knew. He seemed very nice.

    I'm sure he's noble, from some great house;

    His look and manner told you that plainly,

    And who else would speak so boldly?

Exit.

Mephistopheles, Faust.

MEPHISTO. Come in now, in!—but quietly.

FAUST. [*After a silent interval*] Leave, would you, I would like to
    be alone.

MEPHISTO. [*Sniffing around*] Not every girl keeps things so neat
    and clean.

Exit.

FAUST. Welcome, evening's tender dark,

Stealing through this holy spot,
Heart, my heart, learn love's sweet ache,   2730
That lives upon the dew of hope.
Stillness reigns here, breathing quietly
Peace, good order and contentment—
What riches in this poverty,
What bliss I feel in this confinement!
[*He flings himself into a leather armchair by the bed.*]
How good it is to sink into this chair
Where many a one, in times gone by, has sat
Through all life's joys and all of its despair!
How often children must have crowded round
This seat where their grandfather sat enthroned!   2740
Here she, perhaps, pleased with her Christmas present,
Pressed her round cheek against his shrunken hand.
Dear girl, I feel where you are, all is comfort,
Where you are, order, goodness all abound;
Instructed by your own maternal spirit,
Your quick hands spread the clean cloth on the table,
Scatter the sand on the floor, housewifely, in a pattern,
Dear hands, so good, so capable,
That change this cottage into very heaven.
And here—!
[*He lifts a bed curtain.*]
                    I tremble, frightened, with delight!   2750
Here I could linger hour after hour.
Here the dear creature, softly dreaming, slept,
Her angel substance slowly shaped by Nature.
Here warm life in her tender bosom swelled,
Here by a pure and holy weaving
Of the strands, there was revealed
The celestial being.

But me? What is it brought me here?
See how shaken, how moved I am!

What do I want? Why is my heart so torn?   2760
Poor Faust, I hardly know you any more.

Has this room put a spell on me?
I came here burning up with lust,
And melt with love now, helplessly.
Are we blown about by every gust?

And suppose she came in now, this minute,
How I would have to atone for it!
The big talker, Herr Professor,
Would dwindle to nothing, grovel before her.
MEPHISTO. [*Entering*] Hurry! I saw her, she's coming up.   2770
FAUST. Hurry indeed, I'll never come here again!
MEPHISTO. Here's a jewel box I snatched up
When I—but who cares how or when.
Put it in the closet there,
She'll jump for joy when she comes on it.
It's got a number of choice things in it,
Meant for another—but I declare,
Girls are girls, they're all the same,
The only thing that matters is the game.
FAUST. Should I, I wonder?
MEPHISTO.   *Should* you, you say!   2780
Do you mean to keep it for yourself?
If what you're after's treasure, pelf,
Then I have wasted my whole day,
Been put to a lot of needless bother.
I hope you aren't some awful miser—
After all my head-scratching, scheming, labor!
[*He puts the box in the closet and shuts it.*]
Come on, let's go!
Our aim? Your darling's favor,
So you may do with her as you'd like to do.
—And you stand there   2790

Looking like a lecturer
Who fears he'll find, staring across at him,
Gray Philosophy in person!
Come on, come on!

Exit.

MARGARETE. [*With a lamp*] How close, oppressive it is in here.
   [*She opens the window.*]
   And yet outside it isn't warm.
   I feel, I don't know why, so queer—
   I wish Mother would come home.
   I tremble so in every limb—
   What a foolish, frightened girl I am!   2800
   [*She sings as she undresses.*]

      There was a king in Thule,
      No truer man drank up,
      To whom his mistress, dying,
      Gave a golden cup.

      Nothing he held dearer,
      And at the loud banquet,
      Each time he raised the beaker
      All saw his eyes were wet.

      And when death knocked, he tallied
      His towns and treasure up,   2810
      Yielded his heirs all gladly,
      All except the cup.

      In the great hall of his fathers,
      In the castle by the sea,
      He and his knights sat down to
      Their last revelry.

      Up stood the old carouser,
      Drank life-warmth one more time,

Then pitched the sacred beaker
Out into the tide.   2820

He saw it fall, fill up and
Founder in the sea.
His eyes glazed over,
And never again drank he.

[*She opens the closet to put her clothes away and sees the
jewel box.*]

How did this pretty box get here?
I locked the closet, I'm quite sure.
Whatever's in the box? Maybe
Mother took it in pledge today.
And there's the little key on a ribbon.
I think I'd like to open it!   2830
—Look at all this, God in Heaven!
I've never seen the like of it!
Jewels! And *such* jewels, that a fine lady
Might wear on a great holiday.
How would the necklace look on me?
Who is it owns these wonderful things?
[*She puts the jewelry on and stands in front of the mirror.*]
I wish they were mine, these lovely earrings!
When you put them on, you're changed completely.
But what do youth and beauty amount to?
They are not what men pay mind to.   2840
Praising you, their eyes turn elsewhere,
Money's younger, money's prettier,
Money is the thing they seek, all,
Alas for us, the poor people!

OUT WALKING

Faust strolling up and down, thinking. To him Mephistopheles.

MEPHISTO. By true love cruelly scorned! By Hellfire black and
    fiery!
    If only I could think of worse to swear by!
FAUST. What's wrong, what's thrown you into such a turmoil?
    I've never seen you like this till today.
MEPHISTO. The Devil take me, that's what I would say,
    If it didn't so happen I'm the Devil.   2850
FAUST. Are you in your right mind—behaving
    Like a madman, wildly raving?
MEPHISTO. The jewels I got for Gretchen, just imagine—
    A damned priest's gone and made off with them!
    The minute her mother saw them, she
    Began to tremble fearfully.
    The woman has a nose! It's stuck
    Forever in her prayerbook;
    She knows right off, by the smell alone,
    If something's sacred or profane;   2860
    One whiff of the jewelry was enough
    To tell her something's wrong with the stuff.
    My child—she cried—and listen well to me,
    All property obtained unlawfully
    Does body and soul a mortal injury.
    These jewels we'll consecrate to the Blessed Virgin,
    And for reward have showers of manna from Heaven.
    Our little Margaret pouted, loath—
    Why look a gift horse in the mouth?
    And surely the one who gave her it   2870
    So generously, was hardly wicked.
    Her mother sent for the priest, and he,
    When he saw how the land lay,
    Was mightily pleased. You've done, he said,

Just as you should, mother and maid;
Who overcometh, is repaid.
The Church's stomach's very capacious,
Gobbles up whole realms, anything precious,
Nor once suffers qualms, not even belches.
The Church alone, dear sister, God has named   2880
Receiver of goods unlawfully obtained.

FAUST. That's the way the whole world over,
From a king to a Jew, so all do, ever.

MEPHISTO. So then he pockets brooches, chains and rings
As if they were quite ordinary things,
And gives the women as much thanks
As a body gets for a handful of nuts;
In Heaven, he says, you'll be compensated—
And makes off leaving them feeling uplifted.

FAUST. And Gretchen?

MEPHISTO.   Sits there restlessly,   2890
Her mind confused, her will uncertain,
Thinks about jewels night and day,
Even more about the one who brought them.

FAUST. I can't bear that she should suffer.
Find her new ones immediately!
Poor stuff, those others, anyway.

MEPHISTO. Oh yes indeed! With a snap of the fingers!

FAUST. Do what I say—march, man, don't linger!
Insinuate yourself with her neighbor!
Damn it, devil, you move so sluggishly!   2900
Fetch Gretchen new and better jewelry!

MEPHISTO. Yes, yes, just as Your Majesty prefers.

Exit Faust.

A lovesick fool! To amuse his doxy
He'd blow the world up, sun and moon and stars.

THE NEIGHBOR'S HOUSE

MARTHE. [*Alone*] May God forgive that man of mine,
  He's done me wrong—disappeared
  Into the night without a word
  And left me here to sleep alone.
  I never gave him cause for grief
  But loved him as a faithful wife.   2910
  [*She weeps.*]
  Suppose he's dead—oh I feel hopeless!
  If only I had an official notice.
                    Enter Margarete.
MARGARETE. Frau Marthe!
MARTHE.   Gretel, what's wrong, tell me!
MARGARETE. I feel so weak I'm near collapse!
  Just now I found another box
  Inside my closet. Ebony,
  And such things in it, much more splendid
  Than the first ones, I'm dumbfounded!
MARTHE. Never a word to your mother about it,
  Or the priest will have all the next minute.   2920
MARGARETE. Just look at this, and this, and this here!
MARTHE. [*Decking her out in the jewels*]
  Oh, what a lucky girl you are!
MARGARETE. But I mustn't be seen in the streets with such
      jewelry,
  And never in church. Oh, it's too cruel!
MARTHE. Come over to me whenever you're able,
  Here you can wear them without any worry,
  March back and forth in front of the mirror—
  Won't we enjoy ourselves together!
  And when it's a holiday, some such occasion,
  Bit by bit you can start to wear them;   2930
  First a necklace, then a pearl earring,
  Your mother, I'm sure, won't notice a thing,
  And if she does we'll think of something.

MARGARETE. Who put the jewelry in my closet?

There's something that's not right about it.

[*A knock.*]

Dear God above, can that be Mother?

MARTHE. [*Peeping through the curtain*]

Please come in!—No, it's a stranger.

Enter Mephistopheles.

MEPHISTO. With your permission, my good women!

I beg you to excuse the intrusion.

[*Steps back deferentially from Margarete.*]

I'm looking for Frau Marthe Schwerdtlein.   2940

MARTHE. I'm her. And what have you to say, sir?

MEPHISTO. [*Under his breath to her*]

Now I know who you are, that's enough.

You have a lady under your roof,

I'll go away and come back later.

MARTHE. [*Aloud*] Goodness, child, you won't believe me,

What the gentleman thinks is, you're a lady!

MARGARETE. A poor girl's what I am, no more.

The gentleman's kind—I thank you, sir.

These jewels don't belong to me.

MEPHISTO. Ah, it's not just the jewelry,   2950

It's the Fräulein herself, so clear-eyed, serene.

—So delighted I'm allowed to remain.

MARTHE. Why are you here, if I may ask?

MEPHISTO. I wish my news were pleasanter.

Don't blame me, the messenger:

Your husband's dead. He sent his best.

MARTHE. The good man's dead, gone, departed?

Then I'll die too. Oh, I'm broken-hearted!

MARGARETE. Marthe dear, it's too violent, your sorrow!

MEPHISTO. Hear the sad story I've come to tell you.   2960

MARGARETE. As long as I live I'll never love, no,

It would kill me with grief to lose my man so.

MEPHISTO. Joy's latter end is sorrow—and sorrow's joy.

MARTHE. Tell me how the dear man died.

MEPHISTO. He's buried in Padua, beside
    The blessed saint, sweet Anthony,
    In hallowed ground where he can lie
    In rest eternal, quietly.

MARTHE. And nothing else, sir, that is all?

MEPHISTO. A last request. He enjoins you solemnly: 2970
    Let three hundred masses be sung for his soul!
    As for anything else, my pocket's empty.

MARTHE. What! No gold coin, jewel, souvenir,
    Such as every journeyman keeps in his wallet,
    And would sooner go hungry and beg than sell it?

MEPHISTO. Nothing, I'm sorry to say, Madam dear.
    However—he never squandered his money,
    And he sincerely regretted his sins,
    Regretted even more he was so unlucky.

MARGARETE. Why must so many be so unhappy!   2980
    I'll pray for him often, say requiems.

MEPHISTO. What a lovable creature, there's none dearer!
    What you should have now, right away,
    Is a good husband. It's true what I say.

MARGARETE. Oh no, it's not time yet, that must come later.

MEPHISTO. If not now a husband, meanwhile a lover.
    What blessing from Heaven, which one of life's charms
    Rivals holding a dear thing like you in one's arms.

MARGARETE. With us people here it isn't the custom.

MEPHISTO. Custom or not, all the same it is what's done.   2990

MARTHE. Go on with your story, sir, go on!

MEPHISTO. He lay on a bed of half-rotten straw,
    Better at least than a dunghill; and there
    He died as a Christian, knowing well
    Much remained outstanding on his bill.
    "Oh how," he cried, "I hate myself!
    To abandon my trade, desert my wife!
    It kills me even to think of it.
    If only she would forgive and forget!"

MARTHE. [*Weeping*] I did, long ago! The dear man's forgiven!   3000

MEPHISTO. "But she's more to blame, God knows, than I am."

MARTHE. He's a liar! How shameless! At death's very door!

MEPHISTO. His mind wandered as the end drew near,

If I'm anything of a connoisseur here.

"No pleasure," he said, "no good times, nor anything nice;

First getting children, then getting them fed,

Fed all the time, and not just with food,

With never a moment for having my bite in peace."

MARTHE. How could he forget my love and loyalty,

My hard work day and night, the drudgery!   3010

MEPHISTO. He didn't forget, he remembered all tenderly.

"When we set sail from Malta's port," he said,

"For wife and children fervently I prayed.

And Heaven, hearing, smiled down kindly,

For we captured a Turkish vessel, stuffed

With the Sultan's treasure. How we rejoiced!

Our courage being recompensed,

I left the ship with a fatter purse

Than ever I'd owned before in my life."

MARTHE. Treasure! Do you think he buried it?

MEPHISTO. Who knows what's become of it?   3020

In Naples, where he wandered about,

A pretty miss with a kind heart

Showed the stranger such good will

Till the day he died he felt it still.

MARTHE. The villain! Robbing his children, his wife!

And for all his misery, dire need,

He would never give up his scandalous life.

MEPHISTO. Well, he's been paid, the man is dead.

If I were in your shoes, my dear,   3030

I'd mourn him decently a year

And meanwhile keep an eye out for another.

MARTHE. Dear God, I'm sure it won't be easy

To find, on this earth, his successor;

So full of jokes he was, so jolly!

But he was restless, always straying,

    Loved foreign women, foreign wine,

    And how he loved, drat him, dice-playing.

MEPHISTO. Oh well, I'm sure things worked out fine

    If he was equally forgiving.   3040

    With such an arrangement, why, I swear

    I'd marry you myself, my dear!

MARTHE. Oh sir, you would? You're joking, I'm sure!

MEPHISTO. [*Aside*] Time to leave! This one's an ogress,

    She'd sue the Devil for breach of promise!

    [*To Gretchen*]

    And what's your love life like, my charmer?

MARGARETE. What do you mean?

MEPHISTO. [*Aside*]   Oh you good girl,

    All innocence! [*Aloud*] And now farewell.

MARGARETE. Farewell.

MARTHE.   Quick, one last matter,

    If you would. I want to know   3050

    If I might have some proof to show

    How and when my husband died

    And where the poor man now is laid?

    I like to have things right and proper,

    With a notice published in the paper.

MEPHISTO. Madam, yes. To attest the truth,

    Two witnesses must swear an oath.

    I know someone, a good man; we

    Will go before the notary.

    I'll introduce you to him.

MARTHE.   Do.   3060

MEPHISTO. And she'll be here, your young friend,

    too?—

    A very fine fellow who's been all over,

    So polite to ladies, so urbane his behavior.

MARGARETE. I'd blush for shame before the gentleman.

MEPHISTO. No, not before a king or any man!

MARTHE. We'll wait for you tonight, the two of us,

    Inside my garden, just behind the house.

A STREET

Faust, Mephistopheles

FAUST. Well? What's doing? When am I going to have her?

MEPHISTO. Bravo, bravo, I can see you're all on fire!

Very shortly Gretchen will be yours.   3070

This evening you will meet her at her neighbor's.

Oh, that's a woman made to order

To play the bawd, our Mistress Marthe.

FAUST.

Good work.

MEPHISTO.   There's something we must do for her, however.

FAUST. One good turn deserves another.

MEPHISTO. All it is is swear an oath

Her husband's buried in the earth,

Interred in consecrated ground at Padua.

FAUST. So that means we must make a trip there—very clever!

MEPHISTO. Sancta simplicitas! Whoever said that?   3080

Just swear an oath; that's all there's to it.

FAUST. If that's your scheme, keep it, I'm through.

MEPHISTO. The saintly fellow! Just like you!

Declaring falsely—Heaven forbid!—

Is something Faustus never did.

Haven't you pontificated

About God and the world, undisconcerted,

About man, man's mind and heart and being,

As bold as brass, without blushing?

Look at it closely and what's the truth?   3090

You know as much about those things

As you know about Herr Schwerdtlein's death.

FAUST. You always were a sophist and a liar.

MEPHISTO. Indeed, indeed. If we look ahead a little further,

To tomorrow, what do we see?

You swearing, oh so honorably,

Your soul is Gretchen's—cajoling and deceiving her.

FAUST. My soul, and all my heart as well.

MEPHISTO.   Oh wonderful!
    You'll swear undying faith and love eternal,
    Go on about desire unique and irresistable,   3100
    About longing, boundless, infinite:
    That, too, with all your heart—I'll bet!

FAUST. With all my heart! And now enough.
    What I feel, an emotion of such depth,
    Such turbulence—when I try to find
    A name for it and nothing comes to mind,
    And cast about, search heaven and earth
    For words to express its transcendent worth,
    And call the fire in which I burn
    Eternal, yes, eternal, without end—   3110
    Do you really mean to tell me
    That's just devil's doing, deception, lying?

MEPHISTO.
    Say what you please, I'm right.

FAUST.   One word more, one only,
    And then I'll save my breath. A man who is unyielding,
    Sure, absolutely, he's right, and has a tongue in his mouth—
    Is right. So come, I'm sick of arguing.
    You're right, and the reason's simple enough:
    I must do what I must, can't help myself.

A GARDEN

Margarete with Faust, her arm linked with his; Marthe with
Mephistopheles. The two couples stroll up and down.

MARGARETE. You are too kind, sir, I am sure it's meant
    To spare a simple girl embarrassment.   3120
    A traveler finds whatever amusement he can,
    You've been all over, you're a gentleman—
    How can anything I say

Interest you in any way?

FAUST. I'm more pleased by one word of yours, one look,

Than all the wisdom in the great world's book.

[*He kisses her hand.*]

MARGARETE. No, no, sir, please, you mustn't! How could you kiss

A hand so ugly—red and coarse?

You can't imagine all the work I have to do;

My mother must have things just so.   3130

[*They walk on.*]

MARTHE. And you, sir, I believe, you constantly travel?

MEPHISTO. Business, business! It is so demanding!

Leaving a place you like can be so painful,

But there's no help for it, you have to keep on going.

MARTHE. How fine, how free, when you're young and full of

ginger,

To travel the world, see everything,

But soon enough worse times arrive and worser;

No one can find it to his liking

To crawl to his grave a lonely bachelor.

MEPHISTO. When I look at what's ahead, I tremble.   3140

MARTHE. Then, sir, bethink yourself while you're still able.

[*They walk on.*]

MARGARETE. Yes, out of sight is out of mind.

It's second nature with you, gallantry;

But you have heaps and heaps of friends

Cleverer by far, oh much, than me.

FAUST. Dear girl, believe me, what's called cleverness

Is mostly shallowness and vanity.

MARGARETE. What do you mean?

FAUST.   God, isn't it a pity

That pure simplicity and innocence

Should never know itself and its own worth,   3150

That meekness, lowliness, those highest gifts

Kindly Nature endows us with—

MARGARETE. You'll think of me for a moment or two,

I'll have hours enough to think of you.

FAUST. You're alone a good deal, are you?

MARGARETE. Our family's very small, it's true,
But still it has to be looked to.
We have no maid, I sweep the floors, I cook and knit
And sew, do all the errands, morning and night;
Mother's very careful about money,   3160
All's accounted for to the last penny.
Not that she really needs to pinch and save;
We could afford much more than many have.
My father left us a good bit,
With a small dwelling added to it,
And a garden just outside the city.
But lately I've lived quietly.
My brother is a soldier. My little sister died.
The trouble that she cost me, the poor child!
But I loved her very much, I'd gladly do   3170
It all again.

FAUST.   An angel, if at all like you.

MARGARETE. All the care of her was mine,
And she was very fond of her sister.
My father died before she was born,
And Mother, well, we nearly lost her;
It took so long, oh many months, till she got better.
It was out of the question she should nurse
The poor little crying thing herself,
So I nursed her, on milk and water.
I felt she was my own daughter.   3180
In my arms, upon my lap,
She smiled and kicked, grew round and plump.

FAUST. The happiness it must have given you!

MARGARETE. But it was hard on me so often, too.
Her crib stood at my bedside, near my head,
A slightest movement, cradle's creak,
And instantly I was awake;
I'd give her a bottle, or take her into my bed;
If still she fretted, up I'd get,

Walk up and down with her, swaying and crooning,   3190
And be at the washtub early the next morning;
To market after that, then getting the hearth to blaze,
And so it went, day after day, always.
Not the merriest life you can have, sir, here below,
But your supper tastes good, and at night, what a pleasure,
    your pillow.
[*They walk on.*]

MARTHE. It's very hard on us poor women;
    You bachelors are such a problem.

MEPHISTO. What's needed are more charmers like yourself
    To bring us bachelors down from off the shelf.

MARTHE. There's never, sir, been anyone? Confess!   3200
    You've never lost your heart to one of us?

MEPHISTO. How does the proverb go? A loving wife,
    And one's own hearthside, are more worth
    Than all the gold that's hidden in the earth.

MARTHE. I mean, you've had no wish, yourself?

MEPHISTO. Oh, everywhere I've been received politely.

MARTHE. No, what I mean is, hasn't there been somebody
    Who ever made your heart beat? Seriously?

MEPHISTO. It's never a joking matter with women, believe me.

MARTHE. Oh, you don't understand!

MEPHISTO.   So sorry! Still,   3210
    I understand that you are—amiable.
    [*They walk on.*]

FAUST. You recognized me instantly
    When I came through the gate into the garden?

MARGARETE. I dropped my eyes. Didn't you see?

FAUST. And you'll forgive the liberty, you'll pardon
    My swaggering up in that insulting fashion
    When you came out of the church door?

MARGARETE. I was bewildered. Never before
    Had I been spoken to in that way.
    I'm a good girl. Who would dare   3220
    To say a bad thing, ever, about me?

Did he, I wondered, see a suggestion
Of something flaunting in my look?
There's a creature, he seemed to think,
With whom a man might strike a bargain
On the spot. But I'll confess,
Something there was, I don't know what,
Spoke in your favor, here in my breast.
And oh how vexed I felt with myself
To find I wasn't vexed with you in the least.   3230

FAUST. Dear girl!

MARGARETE.   Just wait.

[*Picking a daisy and plucking the petals one by one*]

FAUST.   What is it for, a bouquet?

MARGARETE. Only a little game of ours.

FAUST.   A game, is it?

MARGARETE. Never mind. I'm afraid you'll laugh at me.

[*Murmuring to herself as she plucks the petals*]

FAUST. I can't hear. What is it?

MARGARETE. [*Under her breath*]

                    Loves me—loves me not—

FAUST. Oh, what a creature, heavenly!

MARGARETE. [*Continuing*] He loves me—not—he loves
          me—not—

[*Plucking the last petal and crying out delightedly*]

He loves me!

FAUST.   Dearest, yes! Yes, let the flower be
The oracle that tells your destiny.
He loves you! Do you understand?
He loves you! Let me take your hand.   3240

[*He takes her hands in his.*]

MARGARETE. I'm trembling with fear.

FAUST. Don't be afraid! Read the look
On my face, feel my hands gripping yours—
They tell you what's impossible
Ever to put in words:
Here is complete surrender, and such rapture

As must never end, must be eternal!
Yes, eternal! It's end would mean
Utter despair!
No; no end! No end! 3250
[*Margarete squeezes his hands, frees herself and runs away. He
    doesn't move for a moment, thinking, then follows her.*]

MARTHE. It's getting dark.
MEPHISTO. That's right. We have to go.
MARTHE. Please forgive me if I don't invite
    You in. But ours is such a nasty-minded street,
    You'd think people had no more to do
    Than watch their neighbors' every coming and going.
    The gossip that goes on here, about nothing!
    But where are they, our little couple?
MEPHISTO. Flew
    Up that path like butterflies.
MARTHE. He seems to like her.
MEPHISTO. And she him. Which is the way the world wags ever.

A SUMMERHOUSE

*Gretchen runs in and hides behind the door, putting her fingertips
to her lips and peeping through a crack.*

MARGARETE. Here he comes!
FAUST. You're teasing me, are you? 3260
    I've got you now! [*Kisses her.*]
MARGARETE. [*Holding him around and returning the kiss*]
    I love you, yes, I do!
        Mephistopheles knocks.
FAUST. [*Stamping his foot*]
    Who's there?
MEPHISTO. A friend.
FAUST. A brute!
MEPHISTO. We must be on our way.

MARTHE. [*Coming up*] Yes, sir, it's late.
FAUST.   I'd like to walk you home.
MARGARETE. My mother, I'm afraid. . . . Goodbye!
FAUST.   So we must say
        Goodbye? Goodbye!
MARGARETE.   I hope I'll see you soon.
                                        Exit Faust and Mephistopheles.
        Good God, the thoughts that fill the brain
        Of such a man, oh it's astounding!
        I stand there dumbly, red with shame,
        And stammer yes to everything.
        I'm such a poor little ignorant fool,   3270
        How should I interest him at all?

A CAVERN IN THE FOREST

FAUST. [*Alone*] Sublime Spirit, all that I asked for, all,
        You gave me. Not for nothing was it,
        The face you showed me, glaring, out of the fire.
        You gave me glorious Nature for my kingdom,
        With the power to feel, to delight in her—nor as
        A spectator only, coolly admiring her wonders,
        But seeing deep into her bosom
        As a man sees into a friend's heart.
        Before me you make pass all living things,   3280
        From high to low, and teach me how to know
        My brother creatures in the woods, the streams, the air.
        And when the shrieking storm winds make the forest
        Groan, toppling the giant fir whose fall
        Bears nearby branches down with it and crushes
        Neighboring trees so that the hill returns
        A hollow thunder—oh, then you lead me to
        The shelter of this cave, lay bare my being to myself,
        And all the mysteries hidden in my depths
        Unfold themselves and open to the day.   3290

And after, when the white moon climbs the sky,
Shedding a pure, assuaging light, out
Of the walls of rock, the dripping bushes, drift
Silver figures from antiquity
To relieve reflection's solitary pleasures.

That nothing perfect's ever ours, oh but
I know it now. Together with the rapture
That I owe you, by which I am exalted
Nearer and still nearer to the gods,
Came a companion, one whom I already   3300
Cannot do without, though he's a cold
And shameless devil who drags me down
In my own eyes and with a whispered word
Makes all you granted me to be as nothing.
The longing that I feel for that enchanting
Image of a woman, he busily blows up
Into a leaping flame. And so desire
Whips me, stumbling on, to seize enjoyment,
And once enjoyed, I languish for desire.
                    Enter Mephistopheles.
MEPHISTO. Aren't you fed up with it by now,   3310
      This mooning about? How can it still
      Amuse you? You do it for a while,
      All right; but enough's enough, on to the new!
FAUST. I wish you'd put your time to better use
      Than bedeviling me when I have found some ease.
MEPHISTO. Oh well, a little breather, have it, have it.
      But "ease," man, you can't really mean it—
      I wouldn't shed tears, losing a companion
      Who is so mad, so rude, so sullen.
      I have my hands full every minute—   3320
      Impossible to tell what pleases you or doesn't.
FAUST. Why, that's just perfect, isn't it?
      He pesters me and wants praise for it.
MEPHISTO. You poor earthly creature, would

You ever have managed at all without me?
Whom do you have to thank for being cured
Of your mad ideas, your feverish frenzy?
If not for me you would have disappeared
From off the face of earth already.
What kind of life do you call it, dully moping   3330
Owl-like in caves, or toad-like feeding
On oozing moss and dripping stone?
That's a way to spend your time!
You're still living in your head—I have to say so;
Only the old Dr. Faust would carry on so.

FAUST. Try to understand: my life's renewed
When I wander, musing, in wild Nature.
But even if you could, I know you would
Begrudge me, Devil that you are, my rapture.

MEPHISTO. For sure, your rapture, spiritual, sublime!   3340
Lying in dew and darkness on some mountain,
Embracing earth and heaven in a swoon;
A god no less, so great you've grown, so swollen,
Penetrating the bowels of earth
By sheer force of intuition,
Feeling all Creation, the whole six days' work, inside yourself,
In your pride of strength delighting in—what, I can't
          imagine,
Ecstatically merging with all there is, all being,
The earthly creature transcended and forgotten—
And how will it end, all your exalted insight?   3350
[*Making a gesture*]
I forbid myself to say, it's not polite.

FAUST. For shame!

MEPHISTO.   So that's not to your taste at all, sir?
You're right, "shame"'s right, the moral comment called for.
One mustn't mention, for chaste ears to hear,
What hearts, however chaste, always look out for.
I mean, feel free to fool yourself
As and when it pleases you.

Yet you can't keep on doing as you do,
Already you're a wreck again, sick near to death;
And if you do keep on, quite soon   3360
You'll go mad with fear and gloom.
Enough, I say! Your sweetheart sits down there
And all's a dismal prison for her.
You haunt her mind continually,
She's mad about you, oh completely.
At first your passion, like a freshet,
Poured tumultuously, seething and foaming
And filling her heart to overflowing;
But now the flood's thinned to a streamlet.
Instead of playing monarch of the wood,   3370
My opinion is, dear Doctor,
You should make the little creature
Some return, in gratitude.
For her the hours creep along,
She stands at the window, watching the clouds
Pass slowly over the old town walls,
"Lend me, sweet bird, your wings," is the song
She sings all day and half the night.
Sometimes she's cheerful, mostly she's downhearted,
Sometimes she cries as if brokenhearted,   3380
Then she's calm again and seems all right,
And loves you always in despite.

FAUST. Serpent! Snake!

MEPHISTO. [*Aside*] I'll have you yet!

FAUST. Get away from me, you fiend!
Don't mention her, so beautiful, to me!
Don't make my half-crazed senses crave again
The sweetness of that lovely body!

MEPHISTO. Then what? She thinks you've taken flight,
And I must say, the girl's half right.   3390

FAUST. However far I wander, I am near her,
I can't forget her for a minute.
I even envy the Lord's body

Her pressing her lips, in church, to it.

MEPHISTO. I understand. I've often envied *you*

(she's preggers)

Her pair of roes that feed among the lilies.

FAUST. Pander! I won't hear your blasphemies.

MEPHISTO. Fine! Insult me! And I laugh at you.

The God that made you girls and boys

Himself was first to recognize,   3400

And practice, what's the noblest calling,

The furnishing of opportunities.

Away! A crying shame this, never linger!

You act as if hard fate were dragging

You to death, not to your truelove's chamber.

FAUST. Heaven's out-heavened when she holds me tight,

I'm warmed to life upon her bosom—

But it doesn't matter, still I feel her plight.

A fugitive is what I am, a beast

That's houseless, restless, purposeless,   3410

A furious, impatient cataract

That plunges down from rock to rock toward the abyss.

And there she was, half wakened into woman,

In her quiet cottage on the Alpine meadow,

Her life the same domestic round

Within a little world where fell no shadow.

And I, abhorred by God,

Was not content to batter

Rocks to bits, I had

To undermine her peace and overwhelm her!   3420

This sacrifice you claimed, Hell, as your due!

Help me, Devil, please, to shorten

The anxious time I must go through!

Let happen quick what has to happen!

(admits it but won't stop it)

Let her fate fall on me, too, crushingly,

And both together perish, her and me!

MEPHISTO. All worked up again, all in a sweat!

On your way, you fool, and comfort her.

When blockheads think there's no way out,

Right away they're sure they're done for.   3430
Long live the man who keeps on undeterred!
I'd rate your progress as a devil pretty fair;
But tell me, what is there that's more absurd
Than a moping devil, mewling in despair?

GRETCHEN'S ROOM

GRETCHEN. [*Alone at her spinning wheel*]
    My heart's heavy,
    My peace gone,
    I'll never know any
    Peace again.

    All's a grave
    Where he is not,   3440
    The whole world
    Turned sour, spoilt.

    And my poor head—
    I think I'm mad,
    How it goes round
    And round, my mind.

    My heart's heavy,
    My peace gone,
    I'll never know any
    Peace again.   3450

    I look out the window,
    Walk out the door,
    Him, only him,
    I'm looking for.

    His bold step,

His princely person,
His smiling lips,
His eyes' persuasion,

And his murmuring voice,
Pure magicalness,   3460
And his fingers' touch,
And oh, his kiss!

My heart's heavy,
My peace gone,
I'll never know any
Peace again.

With all of me, I
Strain so toward him,
One thing only
I want, to hold him,   3470

And kiss him and kiss him,
Never ceasing,
Until I die in
His arms kissing.

MARTHE'S GARDEN

Margarete, Faust.

MARGARETE. Heinrich, the truth—I have to insist!
FAUST. As far as I'm able.
MARGARETE.   Well, tell me, you must,
    About your religion—how do you feel?
    You're such a good man, kind and intelligent,
    But I suspect you are indifferent.
FAUST. Enough of that, my child. You know quite well   3480

I cherish you so very dearly,

For those I love I'd give my life up gladly,

And I never interfere with people's faith.

MARGARETE. That isn't right, you've got to have belief!

FAUST. You do?

MARGARETE.   I know you think I am a dunce!

You don't respect the sacraments.

FAUST. I do respect them.

MARGARETE.   Not enough to go to mass.

And tell me when you last went to confess?

Do you believe in God?

FAUST.   Who, my dear,   3490

Can say, I believe in God?

Ask any priest, philosopher,

And what you get by way of answer

Sounds like a joke, pure mockery.

MARGARETE. So you don't believe in him?

FAUST. Don't misunderstand me, sweet girl, please.

Who can give a name to him?

In good conscience say that he believes?

And where's the man who truly feels,

Who has the hardihood to say

I *don't* believe in him?   3500

The all-embracing, all-sustaining

Power of heaven and earth,

Doesn't he embrace and sustain

You, me, himself?

The sky it arches over us,

The earth stands firm beneath our feet,

And don't the stars, looking with friendly eyes,

Eternally mount aloft?

And don't I look at you, don't

Our eyes meet and mingle?   3510

And all there is, all things, don't they

Strain yearningly toward you,

Acting and working invisibly,

Yet visible all around you,
An everlasting mystery?
Fill heart with it until heart overflows
In an ecstasy of blissful feeling,
Which then call what you please,
Happiness or love or heart or God!
I know no name for it;   3520
Feeling is everything,
The name just noise, just vapor,
Dimming the heavenly fire.

MARGARETE. I guess what you say is all right,
The priest speaks so, or pretty near,
Except his language isn't yours, not quite.

FAUST. I speak as all do here below,
All souls beneath bright heaven's day,
They use the language that they know,
And I use mine. Why shouldn't I?   3530

MARGARETE. It sounds fine when you put it your way,
But something's wrong, there's still a question;
The truth is, you are not a Christian.

FAUST. Now darling!

MARGARETE.   It has made me so uneasy
To see the company you keep.

FAUST. Company? What do you mean by that?

MARGARETE. That man you always have with you,
I loathe him, oh how much I do;
In all my life I can't remember
Anything that's made me shiver   3540
More than his face has, so horrid, hateful!

FAUST. Silly thing, don't be so fearful.

MARGARETE. His presence throws me into such a turmoil.
I like people, most of them indeed;
But even as I long for you,
I think of him with secret dread—
And he's a scoundrel, he is too!
If I'm unjust, forgive me, Lord.

FAUST. It takes all kinds to make a world.

MARGARETE. I wouldn't want to have his kind around me!   3550
    His lips curl so sarcastically,
    Half angrily,
    When he pokes his head inside the door;
    You can see there's nothing he cares for;
    It's written on his face as plain as day
    He loves no one, we're all his enemy.
    I'm so happy with your arms around me,
    I'm yours, and feel so warm, so free, so easy,
    But when he's here it knots up so inside me.

FAUST. You angel, you, atremble with foreboding!   3560

MARGARETE. What I feel's so strong, so overwhelming,
    That let him join us anywhere
    And right away I almost fear
    I don't love you anymore.
    And when he's near, my lips refuse to pray,
    Which causes me such agony.
    Don't you feel the same way too?

FAUST. It's just that you dislike him so.

MARGARETE. I must go now.

FAUST.   Shall we never
    Pass a quiet time alone together,   3570
    Bosom pressed to bosom, two souls one?

MARGARETE. Oh, if I only slept alone!
    I'd draw the bolt for you tonight, yes, gladly;
    But my mother sleeps so lightly,
    And if we were surprised by her
    I know I'd die right then and there.

FAUST. Angel, there's no need to worry.
    Here's a vial—three drops only
    In her cup will subdue nature
    And lull her into pleasant slumber.   3580

MARGARETE. What is there that I'd say no to
    When you ask?
    It won't harm her, though,

There is no risk?

FAUST. If there was anything to fear,
　　Would I suggest you give it her?

MARGARETE. Let me only look at you
　　And I don't know, I have to do
　　Your least wish.
　　I have gone so far already,　　　　　　　　　　　3590
　　How much farther's left for me to go?

Exit.

Enter Mephistopheles.

MEPHISTO. The girl's a goose! I hope she's gone.

FAUST. Spying around, are you, again?

MEPHISTO. I heard it all, yes, every bit of it,
　　How she put the Doctor through his catechism,
　　From which he'll have, I trust, much benefit.
　　Does a fellow stick to the old, the true religion?—
　　That's what all the girls are keen to know.
　　If he minds there, they think, then he will mind us too.

FAUST. Monster, lacking the least comprehension　　　3600
　　How such a soul, so loving, pure,
　　Whose faith is all in all to her,
　　The sole means to obtain salvation,
　　Should be tormented by the fear
　　The one she loves is damned forever!

MEPHISTO. You transcendental, hot and sensual, Romeo,
　　See how a little skirt's got you in tow.

FAUST. You misbegotten thing of filth and fire!

MEPHISTO. And she's an expert, too, in physiognomy.
　　When I come in, she feels—what, she's not sure;　　3610
　　This face I wear hides a dark mystery;
　　I am genius of some kind, a bad one,
　　About that she is absolutely certain,
　　Even the Devil, very possibly.
　　Now about tonight—?

FAUST.　　　　　　　　　　What's that to you?

MEPHISTO. I get my kicks out of it too.

AT THE WELL

Gretchen and Lieschen carrying pitchers.

LIESCHEN. You've heard about that Barbara, have you?
GRETCHEN. No, not a word. I hardly see a soul.
LIESCHEN. Sybil told me; yes, the whole thing's true.
    She's gone and done it now, the little fool.   3620
    You see what comes of being so stuck up!
GRETCHEN. What comes?
LIESCHEN.   Oh, it smells bad, I tell you, phew!—
    When she eats now, she's feeding two.
GRETCHEN. Oh dear!
LIESCHEN.   Serves her right, if you ask me.
    How she kept after him, relentlessly;
    Gadding about, the pair, and gallivanting
    Off to the village for the music, dancing;
    She had to be first, she did, all the time,
    And he was always there with cakes and wine;
    She thought she was a raving beauty,   3630
    Accepted his gifts shamelessly.
    They hugged and kissed each other by the hour,
    Till it was goodbye to her little flower.
GRETCHEN. The poor thing!
LIESCHEN.   Poor thing, you say!
    While we two sat home spinning the whole day
    And mother didn't let us out at night,
    That one was outside, hugging her sweetheart
    On a bench, or up a dark alley,
    And never found an hour passed too slowly.
    Well, now the hussy's got to pay for it—   3640
    Shiver in church, she must, in her sinner's shift.
GRETCHEN. He'll marry her, I'm sure he will.
LIESCHEN. Not him! The fellow's no such fool,
    He'll find he likes it in another district.
    In fact he's gone.

GRETCHEN.   But that's not right, it's wicked!

LIESCHEN. And if he does, she'll rue the day,
> The boys will snatch her bridal wreath away
> And we'll throw dirty straw down in her doorway.

Exit.

GRETCHEN. [*Turning to go home*]
> How full of blame I used to be, how scornful
> Of any girl who got herself in trouble!   3650
> I couldn't find words enough to express
> My disgust for others' sinfulness.
> Black as all their misdeeds seemed to be,
> I blackened them still more, so cruelly,
> And still they weren't black enough for me.
> I blessed myself, was smug and proud
> To think I was so very good,
> And who's the sinner now? Me, me, oh God!
> Yet everything that brought me to it,
> God, was so good, oh, was so sweet!   3660

THE CITY WALL

In a niche in the wall, an image of the Mater Dolorosa at the foot of the cross, with pots of flowers before it.

GRETCHEN. [*Putting fresh flowers in the pots*]
> Look down at me,
> Lady of sorrows!
> Pity my wretchedness!
>
> With the sword in your heart,
> Upwards you look
> To your dying son nailed to the cross.
>
> Up to the Father

Your sighs race each other,
For his torment, your torment pleading.

But who is there knows   3670
How sharp a pain gnaws
All through me, through flesh, bone and marrow?
Knows my heart that's so fearful,
Knows how it yearns, trembles?
You only, you only know!

I go no matter where,
The pain goes with me there,
Inside my bosom, aching!
No sooner I'm alone
I cry aloud, I moan—   3680
Mary, my heart is breaking!

From the box outside my window
I picked these, this morning, for you,
My eyes dropping tears as I picked them,
Tears like the morning dew.

Into my room at the dawning
The light of the sun shone red,
It found me bolt upright, sitting
In misery on my bed.

Help! Save me from shame and death!   3690
Look down at me,
Lady of sorrows!
Pity my wretchedness!

NIGHT

The street outside Gretchen's door.

VALENTINE. [*A soldier, Gretchen's brother*]
    Whenever at a bout the boys
    Would fill the tavern with the noise
    Of their loud bragging, swearing Mattie,
    Handsome Kate or blushing Mary,
    The finest girl in all the country,
    Confirming what they said by drinking
    Many a bumper, I'd say nothing,   3700
    My elbows on the table propped,
    Till all their boasting at last stopped.
    And then I'd stroke my beard, and smiling,
    Say there was no point disputing
    About taste; but tell me where
    There was one who could compare,
    A virgin who could hold a candle
    To my beloved sister, Gretel?
    Clink, clank, you heard the tankards rattle
    And voices all round crying out,   3710
    He's right, our Valentine is right,
    Among all her sex she has no equal!
    Which shut the loud mouths up. And now!—
    I could tear my hair out, all,
    Run right up the side of the wall!
    All the drunks are free to crow
    Over me, to needle, sneer,
    And I'm condemned to sitting there
    Like a man with debts unpaid
    Who sweats should anything be said.   3720
    I itch to smash them all, those beggars,
    But still that wouldn't make them liars.

    Who's sneaking up here? Who is that?

There's two! And one I bet's that rat.
When I lay my hands on him
He won't be going home again!

Faust, Mephistopheles.

FAUST. How through the window of the vestry, look,
    The flickering altar lamp that's always lit,
    Upward throws its light, while dim and weak,
    By darkness choked, a gleam dies at our feet.   3730
    Just so all's night and gloom within my soul.

MEPHISTO. And I feel like a tomcat on the prowl,
    Creeping up a ladder, round a corner,
    And how I like it, how it suits my nature,
    Which, as you well know, is rather knavish.
    Tonight I'm itchy-fingered, lickerish—
    That shows Walpurgis Night's already
    Spooking up and down inside me.
    Still another night of waiting, then
    The glorious season's here again   3740
    When a fellow finds out waking beats
    Sleeping life away between the sheets.

FAUST. That flickering light I see, is that
    Buried treasure rising, or what?

MEPHISTO. Very soon you'll have the pleasure
    Of lifting out a pot of treasure.
    The other day I stole a look—
    Such lovely coins, oh you're in luck!

FAUST. No necklace, bracelet, some such thing
    My darling can put on, a ring?   3750

MEPHISTO. I think I glimpsed a string of pearls—
    Just the thing to please the girls.

FAUST. Good, good. It makes me feel unhappy
    When I turn up with my hands empty.

MEPHISTO. Why should you mind it if you can
    Enjoy a drink on the house now and then?
    Look up, how the heavens sparkle, star-filled,
    Time for a song, a cunning one, artful:

I'll sing her a ballad that's moral, proper,
So as to delude the baggage the better. 3760
[*Sings to the guitar.*]

> What business have you there,
> Before your darling's door,
> Oh Katherine, my dear,
> In dawning's chill?
> You pretty child, beware,
> The maid that enters there,
> Out she shall come ne'er
> A maiden still.

> Girls, listen, trust no one,
> Or when all's said and done, 3770
> You'll find you are *un*done
> And smart for it.
> Of your good selves take care,
> Yield nothing though he swear,
> Until your finger wear
> A ring on it.

VALENTINE. [*Advancing*]

What's going on here with that singing?
Pied Piper you, you damned seducer!
The devil take that thing you're playing,
And then take you, you squalling lecher! 3780

MEPHISTO. Smashed my guitar! Now it's no good at all.

VALENTINE. And next what I'll smash is, your thick skull.

MEPHISTO. [*To Faust*] Hold your ground, Professor! At the ready!

Stick close to me, I'll show you how.
Out with your pigsticker now!
You do the thrusting, I will parry.

VALENTINE. Parry that!

MEPHISTO.   Why not?

VALENTINE.   And this one too!

MEPHISTO. So delighted, I am, to oblige you.

VALENTINE. It's the Devil I think I'm fighting!

What's this? My hand is feeling feeble.   3790

MEPHISTO. [*To Faust*] Stick him!

VALENTINE. [*Falling*]   Oh!

MEPHISTO.   See how the lout's turned civil.

What's called for now is legwork. Off and running!
In no time they will raise a hue and cry.
I can manage sheriffs without trouble,
But not the High Judiciary.

                                                    Exeunt.

MARTHE. [*Leaning out of the window*]

Neighbors, help!

GRETCHEN. [*Leaning out of her window*]

                A light, a light!

MARTHE. Curses, shouting—it's a fight.

CROWD. Here's one on the ground. He's dead.

MARTHE. [*Coming out*] Where are the murderers? All flown?

GRETCHEN. [*Coming out*]

Who's lying here?

CROWD.   Your mother's son.   3800

GRETCHEN. My God, the horror, O my God!

VALENTINE. I'm dying! Well, it's soon said, that,

And sooner done. You women, don't
Stand there blubbering away.
Come here, I've something I must say.

[*All gather around him.*]

Gretchen, look here, you're young yet,
A green girl, not so smart about
Managing her business.
We know it, don't we, you and me,
You're a whore on the q.t.—   3810
Go public, don't be shy, miss.

GRETCHEN. My brother! God! What wretchedness!

VALENTINE. You can leave God out of this.

What's done can't ever be undone.
And as things went, so they'll go on.
You let in one at the back door,

Soon there'll be others, more and more—
A whole dozen, hot for pleasure,
And then the whole town for good measure.

Shame is born in hugger-mugger,   3820
The lying-in veiled in black night,
And she is swaddled up so tight
In hopes the ugly thing will smother.
But as she thrives, grows bigger, bolder,
The hussy's eager to step out,
Though she has grown no prettier.
The more she's hateful to the sight,
The more the creature seeks the light.

I look ahead and I see what?
The honest people of this place   3830
Standing back from you, you slut,
As from a plague-infected corpse.
When they look you in the face
You'll cringe with shame, pierced to the heart.
In church they'll drive you from the altar,
No wearing gold chains any more,
No putting on a fine lace collar
For skipping around on the dance floor.
You'll hide in dark and dirty corners
With limping cripples, lousy beggars.   3840
God may pardon you at last,
But here on earth you are accurst!
MARTHE. Look up to God and ask his mercy!
     Don't add to all your other sins
     Sacrilege and blasphemy.
VALENTINE. If I could only lay my hands
     On your scrawny, dried up body,
     Vile panderer, repulsive bawd,
     Then I might hope to find forgiveness
     Two times over from the Lord!   3850

GRETCHEN. My brother! Oh, what pain, what anguish!
VALENTINE. Stop your bawling, all your to-do.
　　When you said goodbye to honor,
　　That is what gave me the worst blow.
　　And now I go down in the earth,
　　Passing through the sleep of death
　　To God—who in his life was a brave soldier.

Dies.

THE CATHEDRAL

Requiem mass, organ music, singing. Gretchen among a crowd of worshippers. Behind her an Evil Spirit.

EVIL SPIRIT. Oh, but it's different,
　　Isn't it, Gretchen,
　　From the days of your childhood　　　　　　　　3860
　　When you used to come here to
　　The altar and, kneeling,
　　Prattle out prayers
　　From the worn little prayerbook,
　　Half playing a child's game,
　　Half worshipping God
　　In your innocent heart,
　　Oh my Gretchen!
　　What thought's in your head now,
　　What crime in your heart?　　　　　　　　　　　3870
　　Do you pray for the soul of your mother,
　　Who by your contriving slept deep
　　To wake into agelong punition?
　　That blood on your doorstep, whose is it?
　　And under your heart, that faint stirring,
　　A quickening in you, what is it?—
　　Affrighting you and itself
　　With its ominous presence.

GRETCHEN. Oh misery, misery!
    These thoughts which race round and round,   3880
    To and fro, in me, in spite of myself—
    If only they'd leave me in peace!
CHOIR. *Dies irae, dies illa*
    Solvet saeclum in favilla.
    [*Organ music.*]
EVIL SPIRIT. The wrath of God grips you!
    The trumpet blares out!
    The graves quake and split!
    And your heart lifts its head
    From its sleep in the dust
    To writhe in the fire.   3890
GRETCHEN. How I wish I were elsewhere!
    The pealing organ
    Leaves me gasping for breath,
    The singing shatters
    The heart in my breast.
CHOIR. *Judex ergo cum sedebit,*
    Quidquid latet adparebit,
    Nil inultum remanebit.
GRETCHEN. How hemmed in I feel here!
    The pillars imprison me!   3900
    The great dome is pressing
    Down on me—air!
EVIL SPIRIT. Hide yourself, try to! Sin and shame
    Never stay hidden.
    Air, you want, light?
    Wretch that you are!
CHOIR. *Quid sum miser tunc dicturus?*
    Quem patronum rogaturus,
    Cum vix justus sit securus?
EVIL SPIRIT. The blessed avert   3910
    Their faces from you.
    The pure souls shrink back
    Lest their fingertips brush you.

CHOIR. *Quid sum miser tunc dicturus?*
GRETCHEN. Neighbor, your smelling salts!
    [*She swoons.*]

WALPURGIS NIGHT

The Harz Mountains, near Schierke and Elend.
Faust, Mephistopheles.

MEPHISTO. What you would like now is a broomstick, right?
    Myself, give me a tough old billy goat.
    We've got a ways to go, still, on this route.
FAUST. While legs hold up and breath comes freely,
    This knotty blackthorn's all I want.   3920
    Hastening our journey, what's the point?
    To loiter through each winding valley,
    Then clamber up this rocky slope
    Down which that stream there tumbles ceaselessly—
    That's what gives the pleasure to our tramp.
    The spring has laid her finger on the birch,
    Even the fir tree feels her touch,
    Then mustn't we, too, feel new energy?
MEPHISTO. Must we! I don't feel that way, not me.
    My season's strictly wintertime,   3930
    I'd much prefer we went through ice and snow.
    The waning moon, making its tardy climb
    Up the sky, gives off a reddish glow
    So sad and dim, at every step you run
    Into a tree or stumble on a stone.
    You won't mind me, will you, begging help
    Of some quick-flitting will-o'-the-wisp?
    I see one yonder, shining merrily.
    —Hello there, friend, we'd like your company!
    Why blaze away so uselessly, for nothing?   3940

Do us a favor, light up this path we're climbing.

WILL-O´-THE-WISP. I hope the deep respect I hold you in, sir,

Will keep in check my all-too-skittish temper;

The way we go is zigzag, that's our nature.

MEPHISTO. Trying to ape mankind, poor wandering light.

Now listen to me: in the Devil's name, go straight

Or I will blow your puny spark right out!

WILL-O´-THE-WISP. Yes, yes, you give the orders here, quite
right;

I'll do what you require, eagerly.

But don't forget, the mountain on this night   3950

Is mad with magic, witchcraft, sorcery,

And if Jack-o'-Lantern is your guide,

Don't expect more than he can provide.

FAUST, MEPHISTOPHELES, WILL-O´-THE-WISP. [*Singing in turn*]

We have entered, as it seems,

Realm of magic, realm of dreams.

Lead us well and win such honor

His to have, bright-shining creature,

By whose flicker we may hasten

Forward through this wide, waste region!

See the trees, one then another,   3960

Spinning past us fast and faster,

And the cliffs impending over,

And the jutting crags, like noses

Winds blow through with snoring noises!

Over stones and through the heather

Rills and runnels downwards hasten.

Is that water splashing, listen,

Is it singing, that soft murmur,

Is it love's sweet voice, lamenting,

From the days when all was heaven?   3970

How our hearts hoped, loving, yearning!

And like a tale, an old, familiar,
Echo once more tells it over.

Hark, the owl's hoot's heard nearer,
Cry of magpie and of plover—
Still not nested, still awake?
Are those lizards in the brake,
Straggle-legged and big-bellied?
And roots, winding every which way
In the rock and sand, send out   3980
Shoots to snare the passing foot;
Tree warts, gross things, swollen, living,
Send their tendrils, dangling, swaying,
Out to catch us. And mice scamper
In great packs of every color
Through the moss and through the heather.
And the glowworms swarm around us
In dense clouds, and only lead us
This way, that way to confuse us.

Tell me, are we standing still, or   3990
Still advancing, climbing higher?
Everything spins round us wildly,
Rocks and trees grin at us madly,
Will-o'-the-wisps, so many, swelling
Themselves up—oh, terrifying!
MEPHISTO. Seize hold of my coattails, quick,
  We're coming to a middling peak
  Where you'll marvel at the sight
  Of Mammon's mountain, burning bright.
FAUST. How strange that light is, there, far down,   4000
  Dim and reddish, like the dawn.
  Its faint luminescence reaches
  Deep into the yawning gorges.
  Mist rises here and streams away there,

Penetrated by pale fire.
Now the fire curls and winds in
A gold thread, now like a fountain
Overflows, and spreading out
In branching veins, pours through the valley,
Or squeezed into a narrow gully,   4010
Collects into a pool of light.
Sparks fly about as if a hand
Were scattering golden grains of sand.
And look there, how from base to top
The whole cliffside is lit up.

MEPHISTO. At holiday time Lord Mammon stages
 Quite a show, don't you agree?
 Oh, you're a lucky man to see this.
 And here the guests come—not so quietly!

FAUST. What a gale of wind is blowing,   4020
 Buffeting my back and shoulders!

MEPHISTO. Clutch with your fingers that outcropping
 Or you'll fall to your death among the boulders.
 The mist is making it darker than ever.
 Hear how the trees are pitching and tossing!
 Frightened, the owls fly up in a flutter.
 The evergreen palaces' pillars are creaking
 And cracking, boughs snapping and breaking,   4030
 As down the trunks thunder
 With a shriek of roots tearing,
 Piling up on each other
 In a fearful disorder!
 And through the wreckage-strewn ravines
 The hurtling storm blast howls and screams.
 And hear those voices in the air,
 Some far-off and others near?
 That's the witches' wizard singing,
 Along the mountain shrilly ringing.

CHORUS OF WITCHES.
  The witches ride up to the Brocken,

Stubble's yellow, new grain green. 4040
The great host meets upon the peak, and
There Urian mounts his throne.
So over stock and stone go stumping,
Witches farting, billy goats stinking!

VOICE. Here comes Mother Baubo now,
    Riding on an old brood sow.

CHORUS.
    Honor to whom honor is due!
    Old Baubo to the head of the queue!
    A fat pig and a fat frau on her,
    And all the witches following after! 4050

VOICE. How did you come?
VOICE.   Ilsenstein way.
    I peeked in an owl's nest, passing by,
    Eyes like moons stared back at me.

VOICE. Too fast, too fast, my bottom's skinned sore!
    Oh, my wounds! Look here, and here!

CHORUS OF WITCHES.
    Broad the way and long the road,
    What a pushing, shoving crowd!
    By broomstraw scratched, by pitchfork pricked,
    Baby's crushed and belly's ripped.

HALF-CHORUS OF WARLOCKS..
    We crawl like snails lugging their whorled shell, 4060
    The women have got a good mile's lead.
    When where you're going's to the Devil,
    It's woman knows how to get up speed.

OTHER HALF-CHORUS.
    A mile or so, why should we care?
    Women may get the start of us,
    But for all of their forehandedness,
    One jump carries a man right there.

VOICE. [*Above*] Come along with us, you down at the lake.
VOICE. [*From below*] Is there anything better we would like?
    We scrub ourselves as clean as a whistle, 4070

But it's no use, still we are sterile.

BOTH CHORUSES.

> The wind is still, the stars are fled,
> The moon's relieved to hide her head.
> Rushing, roaring, the mad chorus
> Scatters sparks of fire broadcast.

VOICE. [*From below*] Wait, oh wait!

VOICE. [*Above*] Who's that calling from that cleft?

VOICE. [*From below*] Take me along, don't forget me!
    For three hundred years I've tried to climb
    Up to the summit—all in vain.   4080
    I long for creatures who are like me.

BOTH CHORUSES.

> Straddle a broomstick, a pitchfork's fine too,
> Get up on a goat, a plain stick will do.
> Who doesn't bestir himself today
> Forever is done for, and so goodbye.

HALF-WITCH. [*From below*] I trot breathlessly, and yet
    How far ahead the rest have got.
    No peace at all at home, and here
    It's no better. Dear, oh dear!

CHORUS OF WITCHES.

> The unction gives us hags a lift,   4090
> A bit of rag will do for a sail,
> Any tub's a fine sky boat—
> Don't fly now and you never will.

BOTH CHORUSES.

> And when we've gained the very top,
> Light down, swooping, to a stop.
> We'll darken the heath entirely
> With all our swarming witchery.

[*They alight.*]

MEPHISTO. What a pushing and shoving, rushing, colliding,
    Tugging and twisting, hissing and gibbering,
    Sparks flying, flames leaping, a burning and stinking— 4100
    We're among witches, no mistaking!

Stick close or we will be parted for sure.
But where are you?

FAUST.   Here, over here!

MEPHISTO. Already swept away so far!
  I must show who's master here.
  Out of the way of Voland the Devil,
  Out of the way, you charming rabble!
  Doctor, hang on, we'll make a quick dash
  And get ourselves out of this terrible crush—
  Even for me it's much too much.   4110
  Yonder's a light has a funny glisten,
  Those bushes attract me for some reason.
  Come along quick, we'll sneak into them.

FAUST. Spirit of Contradiction! However,
  Lead the way!—He's clever, my devil:
  Walpurgis Night up the Brocken we scramble
  So as to do what? Hide ourselves in a corner!

MEPHISTO. Just look at that fire there, brightly shining,
  Clubmen are having a jolly meeting.
  When the company's few, the feeling's friendlier.   4120

FAUST. But I would much prefer to be
  On the summit. I can see
  A red glow and black smoke swirling,
  Satanwards a great crowd's streaming,
  And there, I have no doubt at all,
  Many a riddle's at last resolved.

MEPHISTO. And many another riddle revealed.
  Let the world rush on crazily,
  We'll pass the time here cozily;
  And following what is now the custom,   4130
  Inside the great world make us a little one.
  Look there, young witches, all stark naked,
  And old ones wisely petticoated.
  Don't sulk, be nice, if only to please me;
  Much fun at small cost, really it's easy.
  I hear music, a damned racket!

You must learn not to mind it.
No backing out now, in with me!
You'll meet a distinguished company
And again be much obliged to me.   4140
—Now what do you think of this place, my friend?
Our eyes can hardly see to its end.
A hundred fires, in a row burning,
People around them dancing, carousing,
Talking and making love—oh, what a party!
Where is there anything better, just show me.

FAUST. And when we enter into the revel,
    What part will you play, magician or devil?

MEPHISTO. I travel incognito normally,
    But when it comes to celebrations   4150
    A man must show his decorations.
    The Garter's never been awarded me,
    But in these parts the split hoof's much respected.
    That snail there, do you see it, creeping forwards,
    Its face pushing this way, that way, towards us?
    Already I've been smelt out, I'm detected.
    Even if deception was my aim,
    Here there's no denying who I am.
    Come on, we'll go along from fire to fire,
    The go-between me, you the cavalier.   4160

[(*But first they come upon*) *several figures huddled around a fading fire.*]

Old sirs, you keep apart here, what a shame!
Join the fun or sink in my esteem.
You ought to be carousing with the youth,
At home we're all of us alone enough.

GENERAL. Put no trust in nations, for the people,
    In spite of all you've done, are never grateful.
    It's with them always as it is with women,
    The young come first, and we—we are forgotten.

MINISTER OF STATE. The world has got completely off the track.

Oh, they were men, the older generation!   4170
When we held every high position,
That was the golden age, and no mistake.
PARVENU. We were no simpletons ourselves, we weren't,
    And often did the things we shouldn't.
    But everything's turned topsy-turvy now,
    Just when we're foursquare for the status quo.
AUTHOR. Who wants, today, to read a book
    With a modicum of sense or wit?
    And as for our younger folk,
    I've never seen such rude conceit.   4180
MEPHISTO. [*Suddenly transformed into an old man*]
    My days of climbing Brocken reach their close,
    The Judgment Day, I feel it near at hand!
    And since my cup of life's drained to the lees,
    The world, too, must be coming to an end.
JUNK-DEALER WITCH. Good sirs, don't pass me unawares,
    Don't miss this opportunity!
    Look here, will you, at my wares,
    What richness, what variety!
    Yet there is not a single item
    Hasn't served to do in someone.   4190
    Nowhere on earth will you find such a stall!
    No dagger here but it has drunk hot blood,
    No cup but from it deadly poison's flowed
    To waste a body once robust and hale,
    No gem but has seduced a loving girl,
    No sword but has betrayed an ally or a friend,
    Or struck an adversary from behind.
MEPHISTO. Auntie, think about the times you live in!
    What's past is done, your junk's anachronous.
    The new, the latest, that's what you should deal in.   4200
    Only novelties appeal to us.
FAUST. Am I me, I wonder, I'm so giddy.
    This is a fair to beat all fairs, believe me!
MEPHISTO. Upwards all the witches surge, half crazed,

You think you're shoving but you're being shoved.

FAUST. Who's that there?

MEPHISTO.   Take a good look.

    Lilith.

FAUST.   Lilith? Who is that?

MEPHISTO. Adam's wife, his first. Beware of her.

    Her beauty's one boast is her dangerous hair.

    When Lilith winds it tight around young men   4210

    She doesn't soon let go of them again.

FAUST. Look, one old witch, one young one, there they sit—

    They've waltzed around a lot already, I will bet!

MEPHISTO. Tonight's no night for resting. Come,

    Another dance is starting, let's join in.

FAUST. [*Dancing with the young witch*]

    A lovely dream I dreamt one day:

    I saw a green-leaved apple tree,

    Two apples swayed upon a stem,

    So tempting! I climbed up for them.

THE PRETTY WITCH. Ever since the days of Eden   4220

    Apples have been man's desire.

    How overjoyed I am to think, sir,

    Apples grow, too, in my garden.

MEPHISTO. [*Dancing with the old witch*]

    A wicked dream I dreamt one day:

    I saw a tree split up the middle—

    A huge hole, phenomenal!

    And yet it pleased me every way.

THE OLD WITCH. Welcome, welcome, to you, sire,

    Cloven-footed cavalier!

    Stand to with a proper stopper,   4230

    Unless you fear to come a cropper.

PROCTOPHANTASMIST. Accursed tribe, so bold, presumptuous!

    Hasn't it been proven past disputing

    Spirits all are footless, they lack standing?

    And here you're footing like the rest of us!

THE PRETTY WITCH. [*Dancing*]

    What's he doing here, at our party?

FAUST. [*Dancing*]

    Him? You find him everywhere, that killjoy.

    We others dance, he does the criticizing.

    Every step one takes requires analyzing;

    Until it's jawed about, it hasn't really happened.   4240

    What he can't stand is our going forward.

    If you keep going around in the same old circle,

    As he plods year in, year out on his treadmill,

    You might be favored with his good opinion,

    Provided you most humbly beg it of him.

PROCTOPHANTASMIST. Still here, are you? It's an outrage!

    Vanish, ours is the Enlightened Age—

    You devils, no respect for rule and regulation.

    We've grown so wise, yet ghosts still walk in Tegel.

    How long I've toiled to banish superstition,   4250

    Yet it lives on. The whole thing is a scandal!

THE PRETTY WITCH. Stop, stop, you're boring us insufferably!

PROCTOPHANTASMIST. Now listen, all you ghostly freaks,

    I won't endure this tyranny of spooks—

    Lively spirits are too much for me.

    [*They go on dancing.*]

    I see I'm getting nowhere with these devils,

    Still, it will add a chapter to my travels,

    And I hope, before my sands of life run out,

    To put foul fiends and poets all to rout.

MEPHISTO. He'll go and plump himself down in a pond—   4260

    That's his cure for a bedeviled mind—

    And purge away his visions and his wits

    By having leeches feed on where he sits.

    [*To Faust, who has broken off dancing and withdrawn*]

    What's this? You've left your partner in the lurch

    As she was sweetly singing, pretty witch.

FAUST. Ugh! From her mouth a red mouse sprang

    In the very middle of her song.

MEPHISTO. Is that anything to fuss about?

    And anyway it wasn't gray, was it?

    To take on so, to me, seems simply rudeness   4270

When you are sporting with your Amaryllis.

FAUST. And then I saw—

MEPHISTO.   Saw what?

FAUST.   Look there, Mephisto,
At that lovely child, so pale, so wistful,
Standing by herself. How painfully
She makes her way along, how slowly,
As if her feet were chained. To me,
I must confess, it looks like Gretchen.

MEPHISTO.   Let it be!
It's bad, that thing, a lifeless shape, a wraith
No man ever wants to meet up with.
Your blood freezes under her dead stare,   4280
Almost turned to stone, you are.
Medusa, did you ever hear of her?

FAUST. Yes, yes, those are a corpse's eyes
No loving hand was by to close.
That's Gretchen's breast, which she so often
Gave to me to rest my head on,
That shape her dear, her lovely body
She gave to me to enjoy freely.

MEPHISTO. It's all magic, hocus-pocus, idiot!
Her power is, each thinks she is his sweetheart.   4290

FAUST. What rapture! And what suffering!
I stand here spellbound by her look.
How strange, that bit of scarlet string
Which ornaments her lovely neck,
No thicker than a knife blade's back.

MEPHISTO. Right you are. I see it, too.
She's also perfectly able to
Tuck her head beneath her arm
And stroll about. Perseus—remember him?—
He was the one who hacked it off.   4300
—Man, I'd think you'd have enough of
The mad ideas your head is stuffed with!
Come, we'll climb this little hill where

All's as lively as inside the Prater.
And unless somebody has bewitched me,
The thing I see there is a theater.
What's happening?
SERVIBILIS.   Our next show's starting shortly,
  Last of seven. With us here it's customary
  To offer a full repertory.
  The playwright's a rank amateur,   4310
  So are we all, myself and every actor.
  Well, I must hurry off now, please excuse me,
  I need to raise the curtain—amateurishly!
MEPHISTO. How right it is that I should find you here, sirs;
  The Blocksberg's just the place for amateurs.

WALPURGIS NIGHT'S DREAM

or

Oberon and Titania's Golden Wedding

Intermezzo

STAGE MANAGER. (*To crew*) Today we'll put by paint and canvas,
      Mieding's brave sons, all.
      Nature paints the scene for us:
      Gray steep and mist-filled vale.
HERALD. For the wedding to be golden,   4320
      Years must pass, full fifty;
      But if the quarrel is made up, then
      It is golden truly.
OBERON. Spirits hovering all around,
      Appear, dear imps, to me here!
      King and Queen are once more bound
      Lovingly together.
PUCK. Here's Puck, my lord, who spins and whirls   4330

> And cuts a merry caper,
> A hundred follow at his heels,
> Skipping to the measure.

ARIEL. Ariel strikes up his song,
> The notes as pure as silver;
> Philistines all around him throng,
> But those, too, with true culture.

OBERON. Wives and husbands, learn from us
> How two hearts unite:
> To find connubial happiness,
> Only separate.

TITANIA. If Master sulks and Mistress pouts,   4340
> Here is the remedy:
> Send her on a trip down south,
> Send him the other way.

FULL ORCHESTRA. [*Fortissimo*] Buzzing fly and humming gnat
> And all their consanguinity,
> Frog's hoarse croak, cicada's chirp
> Compose our symphony.

SOLO. Here I come, the bagpipes, whose
> Throat swells like a soap bubble.
> Hear me through my stumpy nose   4350
> Go tootle-doodle-doodle.

A BUDDING IMAGINATION. A spider's foot, a green toad's gut,
> Two winglets—though a travesty
> Devoid of life and nature, yet
> It does as nonsense poetry.

A COUPLE. Short steps, smart leaps, all done neatly
> In a pas de deux:
> And though you foot it very featly,
> Never will you soar.

AN INQUIRING TRAVELER. No, no, the whole thing is a fraud, 4360
> Villains, you deceive me!
> Oberon the handsome god
> Has long been dead and buried.

A PIOUS BELIEVER. I don't see claws, nor any tail,

And yet it's indisputable:
Like Greece's gods, his dishabille
Shows he's a pagan devil.

AN ARTIST OF THE NORTH. Here all I see and paint must lack
Wholeness, harmony.
But I'm preparing soon to make   4370
My Italian journey.

A STICKLER FOR DECORUM. I'm here, and most unhappily,
Where all's impure, improper;
Among this riotous witchery
There's only two wear powder.

A YOUNG WITCH. Powder, like a petticoat,
Is right for wives with gray hair;
But I'll sit naked on my goat,
Show off my strapping figure.

A MATRON. We are too well bred by far   4380
To bandy words about:
But may you, young thing that you are,
Drop dead, and soon, cheap tart.

THE CONDUCTOR. Don't crowd so round the naked charmer,
On with the concerto!
Frog and blowfly, gnat, cicada—
Mind you keep the tempo.

A WEATHERCOCK. [*Pointing one way*]
No better company than maids
Like these, in such profusion!
And bachelors to match, old boys   4390
Agog with expectation.

WEATHERCOCK. [*Pointing the other way*]
And if the earth don't open up
And swallow this lewd rabble,
Off I'll race at a great clip,
Myself go to the Devil.

SATIRICAL EPIGRAMS [XENIEN]. We are gadflies, plant our sting
In those hides which deserve them,
By so doing honoring

Great Satan, our patron.

HENNINGS. Look there, at the pack of them,   4400
    Like schoolboys, jeering meanly.
    Next, I'm sure, they all will claim
    It's all in fun, friends, really.

MUSAGET ("LEADER OF THE MUSES").
    Among these witches I'd prefer
    To linger out my time;
    I know I'd find it easier
    To lead them, than the Nine.

(A JOURNAL) FORMERLY (ENTITLED) "THE SPIRIT OF THE AGE."
    What counts is knowing the right people,
    With me, sir, you'll go places;
    The Blocksberg's got a place for all,   4410
    Like Germany's Parnassus.

THE INQUIRING TRAVELER. Who's that fellow who's so stiff
    And marches so majestical?
    He sniffs away for all he's worth,
    "Pursuing things Jesuitical."

A CRANE. An earnest fisherman I am,
    Above all in troubled waters,
    And thus it is a pious man
    'S seen hobnobbing with devils.

A CHILD OF THIS WORLD. All occasions serve the godly   4420
    In their work. Atop
    The Blocksberg, even there, they
    Set up religious shop.

A DANCER. What's that drumming, a new group
    Of musicians coming?
    No, no, they're bitterns in the swamp
    Monotonously booming.

THE DANCING MASTER. How cautiously they lift their feet,
    All difficulties dodging;
    The shifty leap, the ponderous hop,   4430
    Heedless how they're looking.

THE FIDDLER. This riffraff's so hate-filled, each lusts

To slit the other's throat;
Orpheus with his lute tamed beasts:
These march to the bagpipes' note.

A DOGMATIST. You can't shake me, it's in vain,
Your doubts and criticism.
The Devil's real, how could the brain
Possibly invent him?

AN IDEALIST. The mind's creative faculty   4440
This time has gone too far.
If all I'm seeing's only me,
I'm crazy, that's for sure.

A REALIST. It's pandemonium, it's mad,
Oh, I feel so cast down;
This is the first time I have stood
On such shaky ground.

A SUPERNATURALIST. The presence of these devils here
Is a comforting assurance.
From the demonical I infer   4450
The angelical's existence.

A SKEPTIC. They see a flickering light and think
There's treasure there, oh surely;
Devil's a word that pairs with doubt,
This is a place that suits me.

CONDUCTOR. Buzzing fly and humming gnat—
What damned amateurs!
Frog's hoarse croak, cicada's chirp—
I've not heard worse performers.

THE (POLITICALLY) ADROIT. Sans all souci we are, shift   4460
About with lightning speed;
When walking on the feet is out,
We walk upon the head.

THE MALADROIT. At court we sat down to free dinners,
And now, dear God, there's naught!
We've worn out our dancing slippers
And limp along barefoot.

WILL-O'-THE-WISPS. We're from the bottom lands, the swamps,

Such is our lowly origin;
But now we sparkle as gallants   4470
And dance in the cotillion.

A SHOOTING STAR. I shot across the sky's expanse,
A meteor, blazing bright.
Now fallen, I sprawl in the grass—
Who'll help me to my feet?

THE ROUGHNECKS. Look out, look out, we're coming through,
Trampling your lawn,
We're spirits too, but spirits who
Have lots of beef and brawn.

PUCK. You tramp much too heavily,   4480
Like young elephants.
Step light as Puck, Puck's tread today
Let be the heaviest.

ARIEL. If you have wings from kindly Nature,
Or from your own spirit,
As I fly, fly close after,
Up to the rose hill's summit.

ORCHESTRA. [*Pianissimo*]
The shrouding mists and thick-massed clouds
Lighten in the dawn,
The wind stirs leaves, it rattles reeds,   4490
And all is scattered, gone.

AN OVERCAST DAY. A FIELD

Faust and Mephistopheles.

FAUST. In misery! In despair! Stumbling about pitifully over the
earth for so long, and now a prisoner! A condemned criminal,
shut up in a dungeon and suffering horrible torments, the poor
unfortunate child! It's come to this, to this! And And not a word
about it breathed to me, you treacherous, odious spirit! Stand
there rolling your Devil's eyes around in rage, oh do! Brazen it

out with your intolerable presence! A prisoner! In misery, irremediable misery! Delivered up to evil spirits and the stony-hearted justice of mankind! And meanwhile you distract me with your insipid entertainments, keep her situation, more desperate every day, from me, and leave her to perish helplessly!

MEPHISTO. She's not the first.

FAUST. You dog, you monster! Change him, O you infinite Spirit, change the worm back into a dog, give it back the shape it wore those evenings when it liked to trot ahead of me and roll at the feet of some innocent wayfarer, tripping him up and leaping on him as he fell. Give it back its favorite shape so it can crawl on its belly in the sand before me, and I can kick it as it deserves, the abomination!—Not the first!—Such misery, such misery! It's inconceivable, humanly inconceivable, that more than one creature should ever have plumbed such depths of misery, that the first who did, writhing in her last agony under the eyes of the Eternal Forgiveness, shouldn't have expiated the guilt of all the others who came after! I am cut to the quick, pierced to the marrow, by the suffering of this one being—you grin indifferently at the fate of thousands!

MEPHISTO. So once again we're at our wits' end, are we—reached the point where you fellows start feeling your brain is about to explode? Why did you ever throw in with us if you can't see the thing through? You'd like to fly, but are afraid of getting dizzy. Did we force ourselves on you or you on us?

FAUST. Don't snarl at me that way with those wolfish fangs of yours, it sickens me!—Great and glorious Spirit, Spirit who vouchsafed to appear to me, who knows me in my heart and soul, why did you fasten me to this scoundrel who diets on destruction, delights to hurt?

MEPHISTO. Finished yet?

FAUST. Save her or you'll pay for it! With a curse on you, the dreadfulest there is, for thousands of years to come!

MEPHISTO. I'm powerless to strike off the Great Avenger's chains or draw his bolts.—Save her indeed!—Who's the one who ruined her, I would like to know—you or me?

[*Faust looks around wildly.*]

Looking for a thunderbolt, are you? A good thing you wretched mortals weren't given them. That's the tyrant's way of getting out of difficulties—strike down any innocent person who makes an objection, gets in his way.

FAUST. Take me to where she is, you hear? She's got to be set free.

MEPHISTO. In spite of the risk you would run? There's blood guilt on the town because of what you did. Where murder was, there the avenging spirits hover, waiting for the murderer to return.

FAUST. That, from you, that too? Death and destruction, a world's worth, on your head, you monster! Take me there, I say, and set her free!

MEPHISTO. All right, all right, I'll take you there. But hear what I can do—do you think all the powers of heaven and earth are mine? I'll cause the jailer's senses to be befuddled, then you seize his keys and lead her out. Only a human hand can do it. I'll keep watch. The spirit horses are ready. Off I'll carry both of you. That's what I can do.

FAUST. Away then!

NIGHT. OPEN COUNTRY

Faust and Mephistopheles going by on black horses at a furious gallop.

FAUST. What are they doing, there at the gallows block?

MEPHISTO. Doing, brewing something or other, who knows?

FAUST. Swooping back and forth, bowing down, kneeling.

MEPHISTO. A pack of witches.

FAUST. As if strewing and blessing.

MEPHISTO. Keep going, keep going!

A PRISON

FAUST. [*With a bunch of keys and carrying a lamp, at a narrow iron door*]

 I shudder as I haven't for so long—
 Oh, how it suffers, our humanity!
 She's shut up inside these dank walls, poor thing, 4500
 And all her crime was love, the brave, the illusory.
 You're hanging back from going in!
 You're afraid of meeting her eyes again!
 In, in, delay means death, you've got to hurry.
 [*He puts the key in the lock.*]

SINGING. [*From within*]

  My mother, the whore,
  In the dark of night slew me!
  My father, the knave,
  Made his dinner of me!
  My sister, wee thing,
  Heaped up my bones 4510
  Beneath the green tree,
  Changed into a bird, I sing
  Fly away, fly away!

FAUST. [*Unlocking the door*] She doesn't dream her lover's listening,

 Hears her chains rattle, the straw rustling.
 [*He enters.*]

MARGARETE. [*Cowering on her paillasse*]

 They're coming, they're coming! How bitter, death, bitter!

FAUST. [*Whispering*] Hush, dear girl, hush! You'll soon be free.

MARGARETE. [*Groveling before him*]

 If your heart's human, think how I suffer.

FAUST. You'll wake the guards. Speak quietly.
 [*Taking hold of the chains to unlock them*]

MARGARETE. [*On her knees*] Headsman, so early, it isn't right. 4520

 Have mercy on me! Too soon, too soon!
 You come for me in the dead of night—

Isn't it time enough at dawn?

[*Stands up.*]

I'm still so young, too young surely—

Still I must die.

How pretty I was, that's what undid me.

He held me so close, now he's far away,

My wreath pulled apart, the flowers scattered.

How rough your hands are! Please, won't you spare me?

What did I ever do to you?   4530

Don't let me beg in vain for mercy,

I never before laid eyes on you.

FAUST. It's unendurable, her misery!

MARGARETE. What can I do, I'm in your power.

Only let me nurse my baby first.

All night long I hugged the dear creature;

They took it from me out of spite

And now they say I murdered it.

And I'll never be happy, no, never again.

They've made up songs to sing about me. It's wicked

of them.   4540

There's an old fairy tale ends that way,

But what has it got to do with me?

FAUST. [*Falling at her feet*] It's me here who loves you, me, at

your feet,

To rescue you from this miserable fate.

MARGARETE. [*Kneeling beside him*]

We'll kneel down, that's right, and pray to the saints.

Look, under those steps,

Below the doorsill,

All Hell's a-boil!

The Evil One

In his horrible rage   4550

Makes such a noise.

FAUST. [*Crying out*] Gretchen! Gretchen!

MARGARETE. [*Listening*] That was my darling's own dear voice!

[*She jumps up, the chains fall away.*]

I heard him call. Where can he be?
No one may stop me, now I am free!
Into his arms I'll run so fast,
Lie on his breast at last, at last.
Gretchen, he called, from there on the sill.
Through all the wailing and clashing of Hell,
Through the furious, devilish jeering and mockery   4560
I heard his dear voice calling to me.

FAUST. It's me!

MARGARETE.   It's you! Oh, say it again.

[*Catching hold of him.*]

It's him! Where is the torture now, it's him!
Where's my fear of the prison, the chains they hung on me?
It's you, it's you! You've come here to save me!
I'm saved!
—I see it before me, so very plainly,
The street I saw you the first time on,
I see Marthe and me where we waited for you
In the sunlit garden.   4570

FAUST. [*Pulling her toward the door*]
Come along, come!

MARGARETE.   Oh stay!
I love it so being wherever you are.

[*Caressing him.*]

FAUST. Hurry!
If you don't hurry,
The price we will pay!

MARGARETE. What? Don't know how to kiss anymore?
Parted from me a short time only
And quite forgotten what lips are for?
Why am I frightened with your arms around me?
Time was, at a word or a look from you,   4580
Straight to heaven I was transported
And you kissed me as if you'd devour me.
Kiss me, kiss me!
Or I'll kiss you!

[*She embraces him.*]

What cold lips you have,

You don't speak, look dumbly.

What's become of your love?

Who took it from me?

[*She turns away from him.*]

FAUST. Come, follow me! Darling, be brave!

Oh, the kisses I'll give you, my love—   4590

Only come now, we'll slip through that door.

MARGARETE. [*Turning back to him*]

Is it really you? Can I be sure?

FAUST. Yes, it's me—you must come!

MARGARETE.   You cast off my chains,

Take me into your arms.

How is it you don't shrink away from me?

Have you any idea who you're letting go free?

FAUST. Hurry, hurry! The night's almost over.

MARGARETE. I murdered my mother,

Drowned my baby—

Weren't both of us given it, you and me?   4600

Given you, too? It's you, I can hardly believe it.

Give me your hand. No, I haven't dreamed it.

Your dear hand!—But your hand is wet!

Wipe it off, there's blood on it!

My God, my God, what did you do?

Put away your sword,

I beg you to!

FAUST. What's past is done, forget it all.

You're killing me.

MARGARETE. No, live on still.   4610

I'll tell you how the graves should be;

Tomorrow you must see to it.

Give my mother the best spot,

My brother put alongside her,

Me, put me some distance off,

Yet not too far,

And at my right breast put my baby.
Nobody else will lie beside me.
When I used to press up close to you,
How sweet it was, pure happiness,   4620
But now I can't, it's over, all such bliss—
I feel it as an effort I must make,
That I must force myself on you,
And you, I feel, resist me, push me back.
And yet it's you, with your good, kind look.

FAUST. If it's me, then come, we mustn't stay.

MARGARETE. Out there?

FAUST.   Out there, away!

MARGARETE. If the grave's out there, death waiting for me,
Come, yes, come! The two of us together!
But only to the last place, there, no other.   4630
—You're going now?
I'd go too if I could, Heinrich, believe me!

FAUST. You can! Just say you will, and come!
The way is clear.

MARGARETE. No, I may not; for me all hope is gone.
It's useless, flight. They'd keep, I'm sure,
A sharp watch out. I'd find it dreadful
To have to beg my bread from people,
Beg with a bad conscience, too;
Dreadful to have to wander about   4640
Where all is strange and new,
Only to end up getting caught.

FAUST. But I'll be there with you!

MARGARETE. Quick, be quick!
Save your child, run!
Keep to the path
That goes up by the brook,
Over the bridge,
Into the wood,
Left where the fence is,   4650
There, in the pool—

Reach down and catch it!
It wants to come up,
It's struggling still!
Save it, oh save it!

FAUST. Get hold of yourself!
One step and you're free, dear girl!

MARGARETE. If only we were well past the mountain!
On the rock over there Mother is sitting,
I'm frozen with fear and apprehension!   4660
She sits on the rock, her head heavy, nodding,
Doesn't look, doesn't wave, can't hold it up straight,
Her sleep was so long she will never awake.
She slept so we might have our pleasure.
The happy hours we passed together!

FAUST. If I can't persuade you, if pleading's no use,
I'll have to carry you off by force.

MARGARETE. Let go of me, how dare you compel me!
You're gripping me so brutally!
I always did what you wanted, once.   4670

FAUST. Soon day will be breaking! Darling, darling!

MARGARETE. Day? Yes, day, my last day's dawning,
My wedding day it should have been.
Not a word to a soul you've already been with your Gretchen.
My poor wreath!
Well, everything's finished, it's done.
We'll see one another again,
But not to go dancing.
The crowd's collecting, they don't make a sound.
The square and the streets can hardly contain them.   4680
There goes the bell, now the staff is broken,
I'm seized and I'm bound,
I'm brought to the block.
How it twitches, the skin on each neck,
As the axe-blade's about to strike mine.
Dumb lies the world as the grave.

FAUST. I wish I had never been born!

MEPHISTOPHELES. [*Appearing outside*]
  Unless you come you are lost, now come on!
  Shilly-shallying, debating and jabbering!
  My horses are trembling.   4690
  A minute or two and it's day.
MARGARETE. Who's that rising up out of the ground?
  It's him, him, oh drive him away!
  It's holy here, what does he want?
  Me, he wants me!
FAUST.   Live, hear me, live!
MARGARETE. It's the judgment of God! I submit!
MEPHISTO. Die both of you, I have to leave.
MARGARETE. In your hands, our Father! Oh, save me!
  You angelical hosts, stand around me,
  Draw up in your ranks to safeguard me!   4700
  I'm afraid of you, Heinrich, afraid!
MEPHISTO. She's condemned, she is lost!
VOICE. [*From above*]
                              She is saved!

MEPHISTO. [*To Faust, peremptorily*]
  Now come on, I tell you, with me!
  [*He disappears with Faust.*]
VOICE. [*From within, dying away*]
  Heinrich! Heinrich!

NOTES

Page (line)

1: *Dedication:* Composed in the summer of 1797, when the middle-aged Goethe determined to resume work on his Faust play, the first draft of which he had written decades before, in his middle twenties.

2 (39): *The posts are up.* Manager, poet, and clown are members of a traveling theatrical troupe which must erect a temporary stage whenever there is no building that will serve.

2 (44): *a fix like this one.* The fiction is that curtain time is fast approaching and the company is still without a script.

8: *Mephistopheles.* There is no certain derivation of the name. It makes its first appearance in the Faust legend, in the second half of the sixteenth century.

10 (306): *My good servant.* Cf. Job 1:8. Mephistopheles' betting the Lord that he can seduce Faust is of course modeled on Satan's testing of Job.

11 (342): *Dust he'll eat.* Cf. Gen. 3:14.

14 (437): *Nostradamus.* Sixteenth-century French physician and astrologer whose book of prophecies acquired a European fame.

17 (536): *famulus.* Academic assistant.

19 (597): *seven-sealed book.* Rev. 5:1.

28 (901): *St. Andrew's Eve.* November 29, when "young virgins might have visions of delight" and see their destined husbands.

33 (1063–65): *Red Lion . . . White Lily.* Chemical substances (as poetically named in the alchemical lore) mixed together ("wedded") in a retort.

33 (1070): *young Queen.* The precipitate obtained by heating the mixture and passing the vapor through a series of vessels ("from one bridal chamber to another").

40 (1286): *Solomon's Key.* Clavicula Salomonis, sixteenth-century book of conjurations.

40 (1301–04): *Salamander, Undine, Sylph, Hobgoblin.* The elemental spirits of fire, water, air and earth.

44 (1426): *witch's foot.* The pentagram or five-pointed star, which possessed the power to ward off evil spirits.

51 (1675): *That "there" of yours . . . And that is that.* The pact with the Devil by which the legendary Faust forfeited his immortal soul means nothing to this Faust, who jeers at the idea of immortality.

52 (1716): *A bet!* The old pact is modernized into a bet.

59 (1934): *Spanish boot.* Inquisitional instrument of torture.

60 (1964): *Encheiresis naturae.* A phrase, mixing Greek and Latin, out of the chemical literature of the eighteenth century which Goethe read or heard as a student at the University of Strassburg. It means something like the process,

or working, of nature. After analyzing an organism into its inanimate constituents, chemists not only couldn't reconstitute the living organism, they couldn't begin to account for how life informed and animated the whole. The important-sounding term obscured their helplessness in the face of the mystery.

61 (2026): *No jot or tittle.* Cf. Matt. 5:18.

63 (2075): *Eritis sicut Deus, scientes bonum et malum.* "You shall be as God, knowing good and evil." Gen. 3:5.

65 (2133): *What a man must do to sit on that throne.* What he must do is drink everybody else under the table.

65 (2146): *Brocken.* The highest peak of the Harz Mountains, where the witches forgathered for their sabbath on Walpurgis Night (April 30–May 1).

72 (2348): *free for the taking.* Sorcerers were outside the law.

81 (2600): *Three-in-One and One-in-Three.* Mephistopheles is mocking the Trinitarian doctrine.

88 (2801): *Thule.* Ultima Thule, the northernmost part of the habitable world according to the ancients.

91 (2876): *Who overcometh, is repaid.* "To him that overcometh will I give to eat of the hidden manna." Rev. 2:17.

104 (3272): *Sublime Spirit.* The Spirit of Earth.

108 (3396): *Her pair of roes that feed among the lilies.* Song of Sol. 4:5.

110 (3475): *Heinrich.* The Faust of the legend has Johann for his first name.

116 (3664): *sword in your heart.* The Mater Dolorosa is portrayed with a sword literally piercing her heart. Cf. Luke 2:35.

120 (3761–68): *What business . . . A maiden still.* Cf. *Hamlet* IV.v.48–55.

121 (3795): *High Judiciary.* The court that judged in matters of life and death. It derived its powers from the Emperor, whose power was held from God; against God's power Mephistopheles is powerless.

124 (3883–84): *Dies irae . . . in favilla.* "Day of wrath, day that shall consume the world to ashes."

124 (3896–98): *Judex ergo . . . inultum remanebit.* "When the Judge takes his seat, all that is hidden will be revealed, nothing will go unpunished."

124 (3907–09): *Quid sum miser . . . sit securus?* "What shall a wretch like me say then? Whom beg to be my advocate when even the righteous will hardly be saved?"

126 (3942): *Will-o'-the-wisp.* As a misleading light (*ignis fatuus*) it was associated with the Devil.

129 (4042): *Urian.* Satan.

129 (4045): *Baubo.* A female demon, primitive and obscene, out of the classical mythology.

130 (4090): *unction.* Witches greased their broomsticks with a horrible embrocation to make them fly.

131 (4106): *Voland.* An old Germanic name for the Devil.

134 (4207): *Lilith.* In Talmudic tradition, a female night demon. In Jewish legend and medieval popular belief, Adam's first wife and a lustful witch.

134 (4232): *Proctophantasmist.* A word Goethe made up from the Greek for anus (*proktos*) and phantom. The target here is Friedrich Nicolai, a writer-publisher of the time who had parodied Goethe's *Sorrows of Young Werther* by writing *The Joys of Young Werther.* Nicolai was an Enlightenment rationalist who abhorred all superstitious credulity and overwrought emotionalism. But the enemy lurked within: he himself started seeing ghosts. When the apparitions persisted, believing them caused by "congestion" of the blood, he had his blood let; this was done by sticking leeches on his backside. The treatment was successful. Nicolai lectured on the subject before the Berlin Academy, recommending his science of leeches applied to the hinder parts for dealing with evil visitations.

135 (4249): *Tegel.* A place near Berlin where ghosts were reported to have been seen, cited by Nicolai in his disquisition.

135 (4257): *add a chapter to my travels.* Nicolai published, over a span of thirteen years, a twelve-volume work, *Description of a Journey through Germany and Switzerland in 1781.*

137 (4304): *Prater.* The Viennese amusement park.

137 (4307): *Servibilis.* "One who serves zealously, officiously."

137 (4315): *Blocksberg.* Another name for the Brocken.

137 (4317): *Mieding.* The Weimar court and stage carpenter Johann Martin Mieding, whom Goethe memorialized in a poem on his death in 1782.

138 (4348): *Solo.* These verses of the bagpipes soloist, like other verses that follow, hide a satirical allusion that has proven too obscure for elucidation.

138 (4360): *An Inquiring Traveler.* Nicolai again.

138 (4364): *A Pious Believer.* Count Friedrich Leopold zu Stolberg, who had attacked Schiller's poem "The Gods of Greece" for its "paganism."

139 (4371): *Italian Journey.* Goethe made *his* Italian journey in 1786–1788.

139 (4396): *Xenien.* Satirical verses written in collaboration by Goethe and Schiller attacking a wide range of contemporary German literary and philosophical figures and tendencies.

140 (4400): *Hennings.* One of the targets of the Xenien.

140 (4404): *Musaget.* The title of a collection of poems published by Hennings.

140 (4408): *"The Spirit of the Age."* A journal published by Hennings at the end of the eighteenth century; its name was changed to "Genius of the Nineteenth Century" after 1800.

140 (4412): *The Inquiring Traveler.* Nicolai yet again, but now spoken about, not speaking.

140 (4416): *Crane.* Johann Kaspar Lavater, the Swiss preacher, physiognomist, and religious poet with whom Goethe had a more than ten years' friendship which he then broke off.

140 (4420): *A Child of This World.* Goethe himself.

141 (4460): *The Adroit.* Those who, in the tumultuous times of the French Revolution, altered course with every shift of the wind.

141 (4464): *The Maladroit.* French aristocrats who had held court and government positions and now wandered disconsolately through Europe as emigrés.

141 (4464): *Will-o'-the-Wisps.* Here, parvenus who came up from below, out of the "swamps," in the revolutionary upheavals.

142 (4472): *A Shooting Star.* Such stars were revolutionary figures who rose briefly to the heights of power and then fell.

142 (4476): *The Roughnecks.* The militant people, the *sans-culottes.*

142: *An Overcast Day. A Field.* Goethe let this scene stand in prose.

145 (4505–13): *My mother, the whore . . . fly away!* Based on the fairy tale of the Juniper Tree, a version of which is to be found in the collection of the Brothers Grimm.

149 (4618): *Nobody else will lie beside me.* Infanticides were denied burial in consecrated ground.

150 (4681): *There goes the bell, now the staff is broken.* A bell tolled as the condemned person was led to the place of execution; a staff was broken over his or her head in sign of final judgment.

151 (4690): *My horses are trembling.* Spirit horses, like Hamlet's father's ghost, must vanish on the crowing of the cock.

151 (4699): *You angelical hosts . . . safeguard me.* Cf. Ps. 34:7.